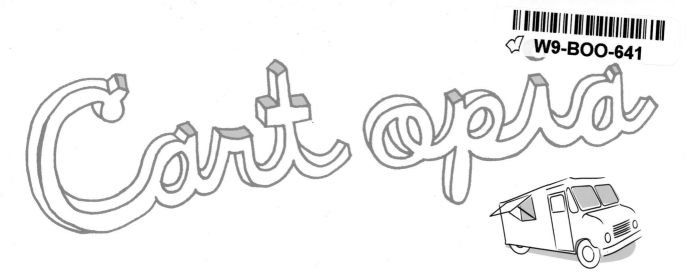

Cartopia

PORTLAND'S FOOD CART REVOLUTION

KELLY RODGERS *and* KELLEY ROY

ABOUT THE AUTHORS

Kelly Rodgers and Kelley Roy have been collaborating on projects since they first met in 2001. Their bond runs deep: sometimes they complete each others' sentences and communicate via ESP. Kelly without the second E can be spotted riding around Portland on her trusty bicycle and Kelley with the E can be seen zipping around on her scooter Petunia. They both emerged from the world of urban planning relatively unscathed and now are making it their life mission to make cool stuff happen in Portland. Kelly without the E is an ideas person and often waves her hands around in wild gesticulation to draw an "air picture" of her thoughts. Although undiagnosed, Kelley with the E suffers from a disorder that does not allow her to focus on doing just one thing; she suspects the extra E in her name may be responsible.

ACKNOWLEDGMENTS

Like many projects in Portland, this book was a result of a collaborative effort. Since we are new to the publishing industry, we are incredibly indebted to dozens of people for the guidance and support they've provided. You may ask: "Why try to navigate the publishing world yourselves, without the wisdom and reach of a publisher?" We decided to self-publish—not that we expected it to be easier or cheaper or to get rich from the famously lucrative book industry—as it seemed more consistent with the way we do things in Portland. Particularly when writing about the Portland food carts, self-publishing seemed like a more fitting approach. More than Do-It-Yourself, Portland's approach to creative projects and social entrepreneurship is better described as Do-It-Together. With that goal in mind, we began by finding our creative partners.

Our first task was to find contributing writers willing to submit their thoughts on aspects of the Portland carts. Carol Mayer-Reed, Michael Reed, Brett Burmeister, and Paul Gerald dutifully completed their assignments and helped frame the content of the book. As a seasoned author, Paul Gerald was also helpful in explaining and connecting us with people familiar with the publishing world. Late in the process, we also recruited Hannah Carlen to conduct food reviews and develop vendor profiles (thanks for your patience while we worked through the writing!). Next, we found an incredible resource in our editor, Christina Henry de Tessan from Girl Friday Productions, who somehow managed to discern a story arc from the incredible volume of materials we gave her—superpowers are the only possible explanation. Photographer Drew Burdick has been so delightful to work with that we dragged out his assignment for months beyond what he he'd initially scheduled. Lucky for us, he is both a patient person, as well as a talented photographer. Then, we found Jen Cogliantry, a wizard of a graphic designer, who nailed the book design concept on her first attempt. Many others helped us with editing, selecting photos, and providing feedback. Thanks to everyone who took the time to interview with us. Your stories shaped the book.

Editor
Christina Henry de Tessan, Girl Friday Productions

Copy Editor
Amy L. Scott, Nomad Editorial Services

Book Designer & Illustrator
Jen Cogliantry

Photographer
Andrew Burdick, Andrew Burdick Photography

Contributing Writers
Paul Gerald, author of *Breakfast in Bridgetown*
Brett Burmeister, FoodCartsPortland.com
Carol Mayer Reed, Mayer/Reed
Michael Reed, Mayer/Reed
Hannah Carlen
Andrew Burdick, Andrew Burdick Photography
Teak Wall

Interviews
Addy Bittner, Addy's Sandwich Bar
Joe Botkins, City of Portland,
  Bureau of Development Services
Terry Brandt, Albina Opportunities Corporation
Matt Breslow, Grilled Cheese Grill
Jason Britsas, Northwest Mobile Kitchens
Supakjanat Brunjongaksorn and Kris Haefker,
  Pbong's Bowl
Sarah Castagnola, MercyCorps Northwest
Kevin Cavenaugh, Architect and Guerrilla Developer
Jonath Colon, Hispanic Metropolitan Chamber
Jack Corbett, Portland State University
Trey Corken, The Swamp Shack
Mike Ebling, City of Portland,
  Bureau of Development Services
Richard Eisenhauer, City of Portland,
  Bureau of Transportation

Alma Flores, City of Portland,
  Bureau of Planning and Sustainability
Bernie Franceschi
Maria Garcia, City of New York
Scott Givot, International Association
  of Culinary Professionals
Charles Heying, Portland State University
Randall Howath, Multnomah County Department of Health
Trevor Hunt, City of Cleveland
Kirsten Jensen, Sugar Cube
Bryan Johnson, Innovision Homes
Gabriela Juarez, City of Los Angeles
Janna Kimmel, 3rd Brain Studio
Jason King, TERRA.fluxus
Ray Koernig, Curbside Grill
Kim Kosmass, City of Portland, Fire Bureau
Mike Krell, Austin Food Carts
Christiane Lauterbach, Atlanta Street Food Coalition
Dave Martin, Oregon Department of Health Services
Marcy McInelly, Architect, SERA Architects
Joseph Readdy, Architect
Shelly Sorenson, Honkin' Huge Burritos
Andrea Spella, Spella's Caffe
Irene Tinker, author of *Street Foods*
Laura Weiss, GO Box
Neeley Wells, Urban Development Partners
Rick Zeidman, Northwest Mobile Kitchens

Vendors
Thanks for submitting your stories. It was so much more fun hearing them in your own words.

Other Supporters
Amelia Armstrong, Amelia Ann Photography
Eric Black, Design Department
Meredith Frengs, Art Department
Ben Hufford, Design Department
Anthony Roy
Jennie Vinson, Mission First Marketing
TENpod Burnside

First published in 2010 by Roy Rodgers Press

Library of Congress Cataloging-in-Publication
data available

Cartopia: Portland's Food Cart Revolution
Kelly Rodgers and Kelley Roy

ISBN 978-0-615-40388-5
Food – Oregon – Portland. 2. Restaurants – Oregon –
Portland. 3. Urbanization – Oregon – Portland.
4. Cities and town life – Oregon – Portland

Cover Photo: Andrew Burdick
Cover Design & Illustration: Jen Cogliantry

Editor: Christina Henry de Tessan,
Girl Friday Productions

Book Design & Illustration: Jen Cogliantry
Photography: Andrew Burdick

Printer: Consolidated Press, Seattle, Washington

Roy Rodgers Press
1315 SE 9th Avenue
Portland, OR 97214

foreword

BY RANDY GRAGG

f the many people, decisions, and, yes, accidents that have shaped Portland's phenomenal food cart scene, the first thank-you should go to Portland's founders Asa Lovejoy and Francis Pettygrove for carving their new town into 200-foot-square blocks. Nobody knows why. One theory is the founders wanted to maximize saleable retail corners. Another suggests they needed to measure some short-yard progress against the unmerciful native flora. But whatever the inspiration, the result was the tiniest blocks of any U.S. city (save for small parts of Boston and Ft. Worth), a nearly 50/50 ratio of building to open space, and an urban DNA that has created a city that is intimate in scale, highly integrated with its surroundings, and, luckily for us, uniquely perfect for the micro-retail phenomenon of food carts.

There are, of course, lots of other factors fertilizing Portland's food cart flowering. And in their book, *Cartopia: Portland's Food Cart Revolution*, Kelley Roy and

Kelly Rodgers have discovered just about all of them, from the rise of Portland's increasingly internationally renowned food movement to the normally rule-happy city regulators' surprising ambivalence about the carts. But the beauty of this book (by two writers who have the highly Portland-centric distinction of being both urban designers and foodies) is that they not only explain the "why" of food carts, but, indirectly, the larger "why" of Portland.

Indeed, the great architect Louis Kahn legendarily chided the city for being "Lilliputian." An equally apt description might be "artisanal"—a handcrafted, small-batch brand of urbanism and civic and economic ambition. Lining the perimeters of downtown parking lots and filling in empty pieces of land along neighborhood commercial corridors, Portland's food carts are the natural extension of the intimate, yet vibrant, ground-floor street experience that Portland has long nurtured (and required on new buildings since the 1970s). They're also an organic manifestation of a local economy with the highest percentage of mom-and-pop businesses of any major city in the country.

Yet, as you read Roy and Rodgers' findings, it's also worth pondering the wider lessons of the food carts. Sure, they are wonderful placeholders as we await an economy that can foster more robust forms of entrepreneurship and development on parking lots and vacant parcels of land. But the carts—and the simple form of social and economic entrepreneurship they represent—could also become a new kind of urban design tool for other cities—and other parts of this city—where the traffic engineers and subdivision developers didn't have the foresight, accidental or otherwise, of Lovejoy and Pettygrove.

As I've watched the carts propagate, first in downtown and later in the neighborhoods, I've often thought of them as the ground floors of buildings to come. But as the carts continue to soar in popularity and develop their own distinctive identity in the city, these busy, Lilliputian acts of capitalism and urbanism shine as a wonderfully exportable form of Portland-style community building.

SALADS LARGE $6

ORGANIC GREENS
ROASTED TOMATOES,
GARLIC CROUTONS,
MEAN'S HONEY VINAIGRETTE

BABY ARUGULA
WITH FRESH BLOOD ORANGE,
RED MEYER LEMON, DRIED
STRAWBERRY, CHEVRE, ALMONDS,
CARDAMOM HONEY CREME FRAICHE

DOUBLE CHIP ALMOND COOKIE $2
ICED TEAS / MEXI COKE $5
BOTTLED H2O $1

CUP $4 SOUPS BOWL $6

ROASTED TOMATO REGGIANO
SMOKED CHILE BRAISED BEEF
HUNGARIAN MUSHROOM WITH DILL CREME

PARSNIP AND GALANGAL

HALF $4 SANDWICHES WHOLE $6

SLOW SMOKED PORK BUTT
WITH PURPLE CABBAGE APPLE SLAW

HAND MADE MOZZARELLA
WITH PARSNIP RAGU, TARRAGON PISTOU,
AND ROASTED GARLIC AIOLI

HERB ROASTED TURKEY BREAST
WITH SPICED BBQ, GRANNY SMITH APPLE
BUTTER, + DOUBLE CREAM BLUE

Part One

THE **PHENOMENON**

> " Lowly, unpurposeful and random as
> they may appear, sidewalk contacts
> are the small change from which a
> city's wealth of public life may grow.
>
> – *Jane Jacobs* 1961

Portland has over five hundred food carts, some clustered into "pods" in parking lots and others staking their solitary claim on the sidewalk. Although some pioneering carts have been serving locals for many years, these quirky little mobile eateries have exploded into a full-fledged urban phenomenon in recent years, drawing no small amount of national press in the process. People across the country are suddenly turning an envious eye toward Portland and trying to figure out how to replicate this unusual model. After all, how many other places can you sample white truffle sea-salted fries, salmon fettuccini, perfectly seasoned pad Thai, and the city's best espresso—all from street

vendors selling from a bicycle, a truck, or even a WWII military mobile kitchen? The trend may be surprising to outsiders, but to those familiar with Portland, the preponderance of food carts makes a great deal of sense. Innovative local visionaries have long encouraged the city's quirky independent culture and creative entrepreneurial spirit. And then, of course, there's Portlanders' love of (some might even say obsession with) good food. In many ways, the food carts are simply the logical outgrowth of all these things—a direct reflection of the city's personality.

Street food has existed throughout the country for decades in the form of hot-dog vendors, taco trucks, and the like. What makes Portland's street food scene so distinctive—and appealing—is the way vendors continually push the genre's traditional boundaries, to the point that entire food cart villages have laid down roots and offer increasingly sophisticated and varied cuisine. These days, in a twenty-minute walk through downtown, you'll encounter a dozen pods of shoulder-to-shoulder carts thronged with loyal customers all happily waiting in line for their favorite dishes. As you stray from downtown, you'll discover neighborhood carts and pods serving a diverse clientele that ranges from waffle-eating families on Saturday morning to after-hours pubgoers seeking comfort food. But before venturing further, let's define what exactly a food cart is and how food carts operate in Portland.

WHAT IS A FOOD CART?

echnically speaking, a food cart is simply a mobile unit out of which food is served to the public. In reality, however, there is a staggering variety of interpretations of this loose definition. While some of these carts are truly mobile, many of the trucks, trailers, and other vehicles sitting in surface parking lots throughout the city only pay lip service to the idea of mobility. Characterized by flat tires or painted windshields, these units clearly aren't going anywhere. In recent years, vendors have become more brazen and ambitious, going so far as to construct awnings, seating areas, and even decks that encircle their carts. Some are cargo bicycles elegantly modified for espresso service or ice cream sandwiches, while others are massively revamped camper trailers outfitted with all manner of bells and whistles, like solar panels or a flaming lotus flower crafted from steel.

DEFINITIONS

STATIONARY MOBILE UNIT
(Theoretically) mobile vehicle with wheels that remains parked in a surface parking lot or vacant lot.

PUSHCART
An entirely mobile and self-contained unit that's wheeled away at the end of its business day. Also known as a handcart.

FOOD TRUCK
The original "taco truck," a vehicle built for mobile food entrepreneurship. Also known as a vending or catering truck.

CUSTOM-BUILT FOOD CART

Food cart built to specification. Can take the form of a custom-built cargo trailer or be built from scratch on a flat-bed trailer base.

TRAVEL TRAILER

A popular and nostalgic form of the food cart, typically a revamped Airstream or other travel trailer that already contains some of the infrastructure needed to cook and serve food.

CARGO TRAILER
Transformed from its drab utilitarian existence by crafty street vendors, this boxy metal cart has been reinvented to serve as a popular form of food cart.

POD
A group of as many as twenty food carts in a vacant lot or parking lot, often with awnings, seating areas, or decks.

COMMISSARY KITCHEN
The food cart version of a commercial kitchen, where food vendors can legally prepare their food according to standard food-safety regulations.

CARTIVORE
A loyal food cart customer. Cartivores often follow their favorite carts via social media.

CARTREPRENEUR
A food cart vendor and business innovator.

CARTITECTURE
The distinctive architecture of food carts. Reflecting a Portland sensibility, food carts often have eclectic and surprising designs.

FREE-RANGE PUSHCARTS

Like many cities across the country, Portland has a number of pushcarts that occupy space in the public right-of-way. Far fewer in number than stationary mobile units (described next), pushcarts set up on certain sidewalk corners and in plazas like Pioneer Courthouse Square downtown. They are fully portable self-contained units with no utility hookups. Since pushcarts lack full kitchens, food is instead prepared off-site in a commissary kitchen and staged for sale each day. At close of business, the carts vanish into storage, leaving no trace of their daytime presence. Although transitory, they are still subject to fees, design review, permits, and regulation by either Portland Bureau of Transportation or Portland Bureau of Parks and Recreation.

STATIONARY MOBILE UNITS

The self-contradicting moniker "stationary mobile unit" describes the many vehicles residing in a more or less permanent location, especially downtown. As long as the food carts are on wheels, they are considered vehicles in the eyes of the law, and are therefore exempt from building code. Types of stationary mobile units include cargo trailers, vending trucks, retrofitted buses, and even an outdoor portable kitchen on wheels beneath a tent. In most cases they have been outfitted with full kitchens; those on the smaller side may use a commissary kitchen to prepare their food for the day. The cart exteriors are often modified with awnings, wood or aluminum siding, painted murals, or other decorative elements to make them resemble tiny storefronts rather than

vehicles. Unlike transitory sidewalk pushcarts, these vehicles remain in place even when the vendors are closed for business. This permanence is more attractive to the vendor, who can thus avoid schlepping heavy carts into storage at the end of the day.

FOOD CART PODS

Ordinary downtown surface parking lots were the birthplace of Portland's impressive street food scene. Just like commuters with a monthly parking permit, food cart vendors rent parking spaces, usually around the perimeter of surface parking lots. Without any regulations forcing them to leave at the end of the day, the food carts maintain a more or less permanent presence at the sidewalk's edge. Together, their walls create the effect of a row of storefronts or other building facade. Some stay in a given spot for years on end, becoming almost as permanent as brick-and-mortar buildings.

URBAN DESIGN & THE STREET FOOD SCENE

One of Portland's original food cart pods is located downtown on SW Fifth Avenue. Almost the entire block between Oak and Stark Streets on the east side of Fifth Avenue is continuously lined with food carts. Complete with awnings, decks, and false storefronts, they give the impression of a classic Western frontier town's main street in miniature. Office workers, bicycle messengers, lawyers, and construction workers stroll up and down the sidewalk to compare menu options, then wait for their orders, all the while serenaded by street buskers. Food choices range from the ridiculous (Brunchbox's Redonkadonk, a hamburger with spam and bacon between two grilled-cheese-sandwich "buns") to the sublime (the lightly breaded Schnitzelwich at Tábor). The Swamp Shack, with moss hanging from its Cajun-styled sign and a deck wrapping around the cart, might win the prize for most expressive architecture at this pod (the 1960s-era office stools don't quite fit the Bayou theme, but the Shack gets points for providing seating).

Food carts, and pods like the one on Fifth Avenue, have captured the imagination of

the Portland public and provoked curiosity about both their development and their impact on the city. A group of Portland State University (PSU) students studying urban planning found the food carts—and their role in activating public space—to be a worthy subject of research for these very reasons. Their study, *Food Cartology*, concluded, among other things, that "food carts have significant community benefits to neighborhood livability by fostering

social interactions, walkability, and by providing interim uses for vacant parcels."

Marcy McInelly, an urban designer at SERA Architects, is delighted with the addition of new carts at the SW Fifth Avenue parking lot. "It's really the ideal situation," she explains, pointing to the cart arrangement. "The carts fill up the perimeter of the block, with only a space big enough for cars to get through to park on the inside of the site." Planners and designers generally abhor surface parking lots, particularly in a downtown location, considering them to be black holes that suck the life out of the streetscape. They prefer buildings, which maintain the visual rhythm of the streetscape and activate it with people. In a down market or on a lot that is difficult to develop, food carts are an excellent interim development measure, greeting passersby with a colorful and

aromatic street wall rather than a line of automobile bumpers.

In fact, one could argue that because food carts, operating from the parking-lot perimeters, capitalize on the edge between the public streets and the private realm, they activate the space in a way that most buildings can't. Standing in line and waiting for orders creates an opportunity for people to connect with other customers and passersby. Food carts actually *encourage* lingering on the street, an activity all but forbidden in many cities today—either by law or as a consequence of poor urban design.

Consider the cities most famous for their vibrant and fabulous street life: European café scenes with plenty of outdoor seating or bustling Asian markets with an abundance of street vendors. In these places, life is literally spilling out into the streets—a desirable condition, noted William Whyte, an urbanist who extensively researched how people use urban spaces. "What attracts people most in an urban place is other people," he says, and food carts contribute significantly to this liveliness. Whyte observed in a New York study that "food vendors were the centers of activity. Wherever they set up their carts... knots of people formed."

William Whyte also concluded that seating is critical for fostering the sociability in public spaces. In addition to helping spark conversation among cartgoers, seating simply makes a huge difference in comfort when you are trying to eat. *Food Cartology* likewise found that seating was one of the most important aspects of a cart's sociability. Carts located in neighborhoods, frequently on vacant lots, have ample space for tents, benches, and assorted tables and chairs. Downtown sites are more constrained in their ability to provide seating, but the more creative vendors have nevertheless managed to shoehorn in counters and bar stools, decks, and café tables and chairs.

Whatever concerns people may have initially voiced about the visual clutter of this

ad hoc development is largely unrealized. Though some people worried about littering or fretted that the eclectic design of the carts would mar the attractiveness of the area, it turns out most people prefer the architecture of the carts to the blankness of surface parking lots or the decrepit look of vacant lots. In fact, some may find the architecture nothing short of stunning—as in the case of a beautifully refurbished turn-of-the-century streetcar named Inspire at Area 23 on NE Alberta Street. Littering has not proven to be much of a problem, even though downtown carts rely on publicly provided trash bins, and the neighborhood carts often have a comprehensive recycling and composting collection

Evolution of a Pod

Pod development over time can be likened to any development scenario: a single cart begins the pod. Like banks and bookstores, the vendor picks a corner spot. As popularity picks up along the parking-lot frontage, more vendors situate themselves in the centers of the block. Others then colonize the spaces that remain between the corner establishments and the carts in the center, resulting in continuously linked carts that form unified pods. Now reaching a critical mass, they constitute a real street food scene, attracting more customers with a greater variety of menus, architecture, and signage. Once established, vendors generally enhance customer amenities in the form of tables and chairs in the furniture zone of the sidewalk. Some even rent a second parking space for customer seating. And voilà! What was once a derelict vacant block or unsightly parking lot has become a colorful and bustling food hub.

system. Strewn with Christmas lights, translucent plastic panels, tarps, bins, murals, and other highly individualized signage, food carts certainly don't create a classically polished and uniform look. But most Portlanders don't seem to mind: "Portland isn't prissy like a lot of places," says Kevin Cavenaugh, an architect and developer experimenting with micro-restaurant spaces. "[People] have a higher tolerance for the messiness of food carts."

Portlanders seem to have an appreciation for the particular aesthetic that food carts provide—or at the very least, are willing to overlook a cart's slapdash design if the food is good. "The interesting thing about the architecture is that it doesn't necessarily reflect the quality of food," Kevin explains. "They might have a dumpy-looking cart, but also have a long line of customers. That's what I look for, as opposed to the physical space, to ensure a great meal."

With varying mealtimes, clientele, and vibes, neighborhood pods have a different feel from those that cater primarily to the lunchtime office crowd downtown. For example, Cartopia at SE Twelfth Avenue and Hawthorne is *the* late-night destination pod of choice after the bars close. Globe lights dangle under a giant white tent, filled with long communal tables packed with midnight noshers. Half a dozen carts serve the predominantly twentysomething

crowd, who come to fuel up on fresh wood-fired pizza, sweet crepes, fried pies, and Belgian fries with artisanal sauces and ketchup. There are even occasionally Dino Tarot readings, where clients choose from a "deck" of plastic toy dinosaurs.

Other neighborhood food cart owners prefer to go at it alone and create their own scene. Food cart owner Matt Breslow leases a quarter block for his Grilled Cheese Grill on NE Alberta Street, a location chosen specifically for its late-night clientele. After the

Laura Weiss & GO Box

One thing about the food carts that sticks in the craw of environmentally minded Portlanders is the amount of waste they generate, particularly in the form of disposable to-go boxes. Laura Weiss is hoping to fix this problem with GO Box. This new business—in its pilot phase as of August 2010—offers downtown food carts a reusable container service. This is how it works: Customers pay an initial subscription fee of $8.50 for their first reusable container when they buy lunch at a participating cart. When they are done with their meal, they return the container to one of several on-site drop boxes, which dispense a special token. The containers are picked up daily by bicycle and washed in a commercial kitchen. When the customer next goes to any participating cart, they hand over their token and receive their meal in a clean reusable container. The cycle begins again. Everyone wins in this case— the earth, obviously, and cartivores (saved from their guilty consciences), but also food cart vendors, who save on their disposable container expenses. You can find out more about the program at www.goboxpdx.com.

bars empty, many of the bar-hoppers line up at the revamped Airstream kitchen to order sandwiches like the Hot Brie, with melted Brie, red peppers, tomato, and spicy mustard on sourdough, or the Cheesus Burger, a burger with grilled-cheese sandwiches for buns. To evoke the childhood nostalgia of grilled-cheese sandwiches, a school bus serves as a dining room—Breslow re-oriented bus benches around dining tables, installed a sound system, painted murals, and covered tabletops with school photos from the '70s. A friendly sign indicates that the dance party officially begins at midnight, although most nights it seems people are too contentedly full to get their groove on.

In the movie-set perfection of the Sellwood neighborhood, five carts are parked in a vacant lot on one of the neighborhood's main streets, almost indistinguishable from the pedestrian-scaled shops nearby. The carts are open for lunchtime and early dinners, and have significant weekday traffic from those stopping by adjacent retail stores. On weekends there's a mixed crowd of neighbors, families, and shoppers that come to Sellwood for its many antiques stores. The pod has a few picnic tables under a tent and a patio set. If a food cart pod could ever be described as quaint, the Sellwood pod would certainly fit the bill. Ray Koernig, owner of the Curbside Grill, understood his market when he selected this location (which also happens to be a couple of blocks from his house). "For street cred, I went with the crisp bright-red cart," he said

Food Carts & Social Media

One of the features that distinguishes a food cart from a restaurant isn't the size of the kitchen, as you might expect, but the extent to which food carts rely on social media as a marketing tool. Many food cart vendors are very savvy about exploring new ways to market their carts and connect with their customers through Twitter and Facebook. For instance, Koi Fusion, the roving Korean-Mexican taco truck (officially blessed by their L.A. inspiration, Kogi BBQ), tweets their location so fans can find them.

Since most carts aren't actually mobile, they use social media to keep cartivores up to date about specials or fundraisers they are having. Thanks to Twitter, plenty of Portlanders knew all about Greg Abbot's cart, Whiffie's, well before it even opened. Greg had very cleverly harnessed the technology to build up a collective yearning for pies, and the ploy clearly worked. Whether he's partnering with the community to do a fundraising pie-eating contest or checking in with his customers via Twitter or Facebook, Greg is a great example of the new generation of cart owners who are using the Internet to build loyalty and spread the word. There's no need for food carts to rely on traditional press or to pay good money for PR when most of their clientele are so tech savvy.

about his shiny cargo trailer. "A funky renovated Airstream—as cool as I think they are—was not going to work in this neighborhood." Rather than a tacked-on feature, food carts are proving to be as much a reflection of neighborhood character as any other local business.

Many vendors are drawn to the social aspect of street vending. Cart owners appreciate building relationships with their customers, something that is difficult to accomplish with a restaurant. Neeley Wells of Urban Development Partners, who is developing a food cart pod on SE Belmont Street, noted that cooks often face a dilemma in the restaurant business. "If you cook, you don't get to interact with customers; if you work the front, you don't get to cook." Food carts offer an alternative—and evidently it's one that cooks very much desire.

Kirsten Jensen opened Sugar Cube, a dessert cart, after several years in the restaurant business. She says one of the best things about owning a cart is the direct connection with customers. Her goal is to introduce her customers to new flavor experiences, so she often gives away samples of her latest concoction. "Some of my regulars stick to chocolate or vanilla," she explains, "but I give them a sample of something different and

we talk about it." Addy Bittner is another food cart owner who is happy with the social aspect of the business: "It's fun to establish a relationship with regular customers and neighboring cart owners," she said. Addy, for instance, has struck up a friendship with Mohammed at the cart next door, Ugarit Mediterranean Meals: "Sometimes we'll share a beer or he'll make food for everyone."

Joseph Readdy, an architect and urban designer who eats and tweets his food cart meals, has observed the very personal level of service that food carts provide. "The interface between the customer and the cart owner is open, direct, and intimate. Lots of places have recognized me the second time that I've been back to their cart," says Joseph. "You rarely get that at a more formal restaurant. There is an informality to the interaction between customer and chef—or between the customers in line—that doesn't exist in a restaurant setting." As an example, he recounted an experience from December 2009. In line at Parkers Waffles, "The customer behind me and I started talking about food carts and cart food. It happened to be exactly the ten-year anniversary of the day that I first met the woman

that became my wife at a taco stand. I told her the story of our meeting and courtship and how it got me to move from Oakland to Portland. It was one of those sweet stories that you can share with strangers to pass the time—except that on my very next visit to Parkers Waffles, the owner not only recalled my visit and the story, but shared it with all of the other waiting customers."

Andrea Spella has owned a cart at SW Ninth and Alder for four years and recently opened a café on SW Fifth Avenue. He knows his customers and their orders, and talks with them while pulling their espresso shots or serving *affogato* (a shot of espresso

poured over ice cream). Bernie Franceschi, a lover of espresso and supporter of Spella's Caffe, appreciates the care that Andrea puts into his coffee (he roasts his own) and his customers. "I once asked one of his new hires how it was going," said Bernie. "He responded that he was learning to pull a shot, but the hardest thing was to remember everyone's name." What Andrea understands, Bernie explains, is how important rapport with the customer is in terms of the quality of the customer experience. And people do indeed love the carts. It's not just the food—which some report as "exceptionally good" or "some of the best food I've had in my entire life"—but the whole atmosphere that keeps customers waiting in line for the latest delicacy. Some cartivores report that the carts "feel very communal" and that it provides them an opportunity to see their neighbors frequently. The casual atmosphere is welcoming to families and those with dogs. Neeley Wells from Urban Development Partners feels that food carts provide a truly relaxed environment. "I didn't want to go through eight years of not eating out when I had a child," says Neeley. "And, at the carts,

I can get something I want, and my kid can get something that she wants. It's fun to eat different food at the same place." Additionally, cartgoers appreciate the opportunity to support business owners directly, and to develop a relationship with them.

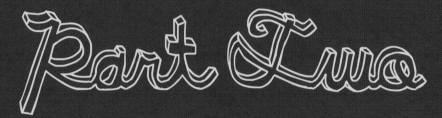

WHY **HERE**? WHY **NOW**?

❝ Food vendors have been the caterers of the outdoor life of the city…❞

— William Whyte

ome of the key ingredients for Portland's food cart revolution are found in its culture. When people think of Portland, they often associate it with a high quality of life. It's well known for its big-city amenities and small-town charm, its bikable streets and walkable small city blocks, its proximity to the mountains and the coast, its handcrafted beers, and its dedication to local food. Portland's culture can be described as democratic and accessible—it's a place that has become famous for its "virtuous cycle of civic engagement." Portland also has a creative independent streak that often takes the form of budget-minded do-it-yourself projects and artisanal craftsmanship. It's no surprise that the stars aligned for a food cart revolution in Portland. When you consider locals' love of high-quality food, their creative entrepreneurship, and appreciation of good value, the fact that food carts took off here is actually quite logical.

While Portland's culture helped to generate the ingenuity of great food carts and the public's enthusiastic response to them, one can't ignore another critical ingredient: the bureaucratic ease of starting a cart in Portland. Portland's street vendors are not burdened by excessive red tape (at least on private property), and business start-up costs are much lower compared to those in other U.S. cities. Finally, the City's willingness to turn a blind eye toward the ambiguous and loose interpretations of the term "vehicle" has enabled Portland food carts to multiply far beyond their counterparts in other cities.

Finally, if cart-friendly regulations laid the legal foundation, and Portland's culture provided the inspiration, then it is certainly the economy that has fueled food carts' recent growth. As the unemployed get creative about their livelihood in the current economic

Greek
garlic sauce,
tomato, artichoke
heart, olive, red
onion, feta cheese
$3.50

Margera

Kitchen Sink
red sauce and just
about everything
else I can find
$3.50

climate, food carts are thriving. An *Oregon Business* article noted that "Portland's ubiquitous food carts provide more than great food at a bargain. With low operating costs and the lure of self-employment, hundreds of immigrants, chefs, and first-time business owners have turned to food carts as recession-busting businesses."

Before we delve any further into the history of food carts in Portland, we'd like to acknowledge that we're well aware that Portland didn't invent the food cart phenomenon.

Portland is neither Tokyo, Bangkok, nor Taipei. In many countries and cities, street food is abundant and the cart business is an integral part of their informal economies. However, Portland's recent ranking as the top destination for street food by CNN/*Budget Travel* demonstrates that Portland is giving these places a run for their money. While the street food scene in Thailand, Singapore, or India may score higher points for vibrancy, Portland's food cart scene offers a combination of diversity, quality, and value that is hard to beat.

A QUICK HISTORY

Portland's first modern food cart arrived in 1965, courtesy of Maury Dragoon, who began selling kosher hot dogs from a Hebrew National cart across from City Hall. He offered the mayor and his staff free samples of his lunchtime fare. The mayor accepted—and in doing so legitimized the food cart industry in Portland and laid the political foundation for their success today.

When Pioneer Courthouse Square—affectionately known as "Portland's living room"—was built in 1984, food carts were a planned feature for the space. Over time, additional carts staked out their turf on nearby sidewalks, and some went so far as to rent space from surface parking lots. At first, the Portland cart scene was not unlike that of other American cities—tacos, burritos, hot dogs, and Thai food were common staples. The carts weren't fancy; vendors were mostly just trying to get by. The number of food carts steadily grew,

however, both in the downtown core and in the surrounding neighborhoods. Parking-lot owners realized that leasing space to food carts was a good business strategy, since a food cart tenant could generate about 50% more revenue than a parked car.

In the past decade, the food on offer began to change, with an influx of artisan carts and new ideas emerging as competition increased and vendors presented unique offerings. Inventive grilled-cheese sandwiches, artisanal soups, vegetarian and vegan options, breakfast, and late-night fare became available. Many cart owners designed elaborate carts with impressive kitchens, which enabled them to prepare more sophisticated dishes. Portland carts spilled out of the confines of downtown in greater numbers and began to colonize patches in

neighborhoods throughout the city. These new carts and their owners breathed new life into the already thriving food cart scene, and people outside the city began to take note. Portland food carts suddenly became a media darling, garnering coverage in such publications as *Details*, *Gourmet*, the *New York Times*, *Sunset magazine*, and *Everyday with Rachael Ray*. As word spread, Portland food carts became the envy of many cities, hailed as a model from places as disparate as Atlanta, Toronto, and New York City.

CODE & CITY GOVERNMENT

Hailed by urbanists as purveyors of street liveliness, community-building, and creative architectural expression, food carts warm the city-lover's heart while filling her belly. But what does the City make of this ad hoc phenomenon?

In the mid-1990s, the City had some concern about the quality and safety of the pushcarts. Jeff Joslin, then lead urban designer at the City of Portland, and others created modest prescriptive design regulations for pushcarts that addressed a range of issues, such as how big the cart footprint could be, its distance to the corner, the size of umbrellas, and the cart's ability to hide its tanks and other unsightly equipment. Reflecting back on that work, Jeff feels that they were able to "raise the bar" of pushcart design. As for the carts on private property, Jeff has mixed feelings: "They can be either wonderfully chaotic or disturbingly junky, depending on who you are or how you are feeling that day. I've been on all ends of the spectrum myself." On raising the bar of parked cart design, he says: "I'm not holding my breath for the City to lead that charge."

Indeed, when asked about the City's role in food cart proliferation, Joe Botkins from the Bureau of Development Services responds flatly that they "ignore them." Because food carts are considered vehicles (whether or not they are actually mobile), the building-code officers don't have much say in their regulation on private property (they have some say in the construction of decks and awnings and the disposal of wastewater, but that's about it). Code officials get a little nervous about the number of propane tanks on-site or

how the carts are electrically wired (not entirely without reason, it turns out, as a propane tank did once explode at the PSU pod early one morning; thankfully, no one was hurt).

There are probably other issues the City could choose to enforce if it so desired. However, Portland City code compliance is complaint driven; that is, they are not out looking for problems. As long as the community supports food carts, the City just leaves well enough alone. And while some of the planning and permit staff may grumble about the light regulation of food carts, they are also frequent visitors to the bustling pod in the parking lot across from their office building.

Regulations for food trucks parked in the public right-of-way (on public streets, sidewalks, or public squares) aren't so different than those in most cities, and these carts face much more regulation than carts parked on private property; as a result there are fewer than twenty carts in the public right-of-way and only one cart in a City park. The key, therefore, is to park on private property, where cart owners need not worry about feeding a meter in a parking space, nor concern themselves with extra red tape.

The Multnomah County Environmental Health inspectors, on the other hand, are more active in monitoring the carts with regard to food-safety issues. In 1997, Oregon

consolidated its food cart and restaurant code sections into one, thereby regulating food carts as restaurants (for the most part). As a result, from the perspective of the Multnomah County Health Department, a food cart is essentially a restaurant. Carts aren't exactly restaurants, of course—they don't have the benefit of plumbing, for example, so most vendors must tote in the minimum requirement of thirty-five gallons of water for cooking and another forty or more gallons for cleaning. Nonetheless, while the logistical operations of a cart are markedly different from those of a restaurant, the food-safety rules are largely the same.

Although vendors in other cities are trying to push for more lenient food cart regulations, their red tape, for now, remains an obstacle. In New York City, street vendors are routinely hassled by police, sometimes for no clear reason. Sean Basinkski, the executive director of the Street Vendor Project in New York City, observed that,

"Portland, Oregon has over two times as many street-food vendors per capita as New York City, and they're doing it better out there in large part because there's less bureaucracy." In an interview about Portland food carts with the *Toronto Sun*, Portland mayor Sam Adams confirmed, "We have worked really hard to stay the hell out of the way."

Los Angeles is another city that's battling for more cart rights. Street food vendors banded together in 2008 and successfully sued the City and County of Los Angeles for their onerous regulations with regard to the food truck industry. A roving food truck vendor announcing his locations via Twitter caught on as a clever and fun phenomenon (one that was even mimicked in Portland), but the practice was actually created partly out of necessity. In Los Angeles, food trucks park in metered spaces and face strict fines for exceeding the time limit of their space. They aren't welcome in front of established four-star restaurants, whose owners frequently harass cart operators. So they are constantly on the move—and keep their fans abreast of their location with twenty-first-century technological savvy. The City of Los Angeles is now under directive from the mayor to figure out how to manage food trucks, which remain popular with the public despite the regulations and negative stigma.

Other cities have food cart aspirations as well, and interest groups and task forces have formed to study how to remove regulatory barriers. Christiane Lauterbach of the Atlanta Street Food Coalition finds Portland's food cart scene "inspiring" and bemoans the lack of carts in her home city. To raise awareness on the wonders of mobile vending, the coalition stages "urban picnics" in parking lots around Atlanta. And despite the fact that Marination Mobile of Seattle won *Good Morning America's* food cart competition, Seattle's street food scene has struggled. Victims of a seven-year ban on food carts, mobile eateries have only recently begun to emerge as a real trend now that Seattle is re-examining its city codes.

If food carts are so great, should the City be doing more to support them? Should more effort be made to encourage their development, in Portland or elsewhere? Brett Burmeister, who tracks food cart developments on FoodCartsPortland.com, cautions against too much enthusiasm for the carts: "If too many people think about how to encourage food carts, it could lead to over-regulation, which would increase costs," says Brett. "Keep it simple. Otherwise, we could damage what made them great in the first place." Alma Flores from the Bureau of Planning and Sustainability believes that supporting the food carts does not need to be complicated. She also notes that the success of food carts in Portland doesn't mean that it will work in other places. What works for Portland might not be the solution elsewhere, but it's an interesting model that certainly suggests possibilities.

PORTLAND'S DISTINCTIVE FOOD SCENE

High on Portland's list of quality-of-life indicators is good food. A 2007 *New York Times* article noted the recent evolution of Portland's culinary scene, lauding it as a "golden age of eating and drinking." According to the past president of the International Association of Culinary Professionals (IACP), Scott Givot, Portland is at the leading edge of the nation's culinary arts.

Although "local" and "sustainable" are popular buzz words around the country these days, Portlanders have taken this concept to heart in a big way. The city's culinary scene is defined by a visceral commitment to local and sustainable foods, exemplified by the long list of member restaurants in the sustainability-focused Chef's Collaborative.

Another defining feature of the Portland culinary scene is that it doesn't come with an elitist attitude. Portlanders are vehemently democratic about food, believing that a good meal can be found in a dive joint as much as a four-star restaurant. Street food is so accepted here that the carts are granted their own awards by the local papers. In some instances, food reviewers don't even distinguish between food cart and restaurant fare when dishing out kudos.

The annual conference of the IACP was held in Portland in 2010, citing Portland's tremendous growth in culinary skill in the past ten years, with exceptional craft in meat and cheese production as well as restaurant fare. In fact, judges at the sold-out Eat Mobile festival, which organizers timed in concert with the IACP conference, were pulled from IACP's board. Judges were delighted with what they found. Scott Givot, one of the judges, reported:

"It is at once a compelling and engaging thought to embrace that such affordable

and delicious gastronomic delights are available to the teeming population of Portland. Even more amazing is the model, which has been created to provide entrepreneurs with a unique microenterprise to support an individual's and family economy, particularly in respect to immigrant populations. Food heritage is clearly a source of pride and it is manifested throughout the city in a spectacular rainbow of tastes, aroma, and color. In addition, it invites the public to walk during their lunch breaks and welcomes the opportunity to engage in the community. How I long for this opportunity in my home of Oslo, Norway!

I was honored to serve as a judge for Willamette Week Eat Mobile Food Cart Festival. I was astounded that at every single one of the food carts from which I enjoyed a "taste"

(and there were 30, mind you!), not one person that was asked for the origin of the meat was unable to identify the source of the product. Now if THAT isn't testimonial evidence as to why Portland is regarded as the new Mecca of the US, not only in the culinary world and its food systems, I don't know what is."

This brings us to another important point: Portland food cart vendors are constantly pushing the boundaries of what constitutes street food. New vendors include those who have just graduated from culinary school and others who have defected to food carts after many frustrating years of work in the restaurant industry. Bringing some serious culinary chops to the local street food scene, they're eager to experiment. One example is Addy Bittner, a Western Culinary Institute graduate; her eponymous food cart downtown serves gastronomical delights not likely to be found in most food carts around the country, like a duck confit sandwich with cranberry relish.

With some items hitting an $8 mark (considered high in the food cart world), carts are no longer just about bargain food. Brett Burmeister of FoodCartsPortland.com argues

that the price isn't the point, though. "You can still get a perfectly good lunch—say, an Indian meal—for $5. But some of the newer carts are offering something unique. They offer handcrafted food—some with meat raised within fifty miles of here—and people are willing to pay a couple extra dollars for it." Skeptics think that grabbing an $8 meal from a food cart without the luxury of seating and shelter from the elements is pushing the limits of what the market will support. But Kevin Cavenaugh believes haute cuisine and bargain fare can coexist. "There's room for all of them," Kevin explains. "If someone is selling the $8 sandwich, someone else will set up $2 pizza next door. The market can and will absorb all

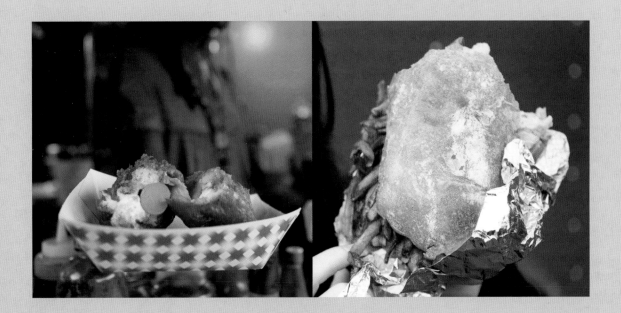

that." Jonath Colon of the Hispanic Metropolitan Chamber works with many small business owners, including immigrants who are venturing into the food cart industry. He says that gourmet carts have their place, and echoes the sentiment that the market will prove out the business model. However, Jonath emphasizes that "people in Portland value quality, quantity, and affordable price points."

While many newer vendors favor haute cuisine these days, others are taking their offerings in an altogether different direction, showcasing fare that can only be called ridiculous or gluttonous. Some of these hefty creations are intended as a hearty lunchtime meal, while others are crafted as late-night snacks. Big-Ass Sandwiches include a choice of meat and a half pound of french fries—on the sandwich. At Stevie's Chicken and Waffles, you can order a deep-fried, bacon-wrapped Twinkie with a hot dog inside, or opt for the fried chicken breast wrapped in a peanut butter–slathered waffle. After Greg Abbot of Whiffie's experimented with a pie machine, he immediately identified the target market for his fried-pie creations: "Drunk people will eat this," he thought—and indeed they do. No doubt that same clientele supports quite a few of the other more peculiar culinary creations served out of carts. While it might appear that this trend represents the polar opposite of the refined fare mentioned earlier, it's simply consistent with Portland's food democracy—prepare something delicious, and the people will come.

PORTLAND'S FAMED LIVABILITY

Portland is an attractive place to live. As Carl Abbott, a Portland State University professor, notes in his book *Greater Portland*, "Many people think that Portland is at its best in the small pleasures: downtown squares and streetcar-era shopping districts, fountains and parks, coffeehouses and microbreweries, bookstores and bike paths..." But the charmed life in Portland is no accident. Locals came together in the 1960s to fight for the removal of a highway from the waterfront, and in the process they launched a tradition of neighborhood activism with far-reaching consequences. Since then, Portland has consistently voted for neighborhoods over freeways, parks over cars, and civic spaces over gated communities. This history of community spirit was described as a "positive

epidemic of civic engagement" by Robert Putnam, author of the books *Bowling Alone* and *Better Together*. Place matters dearly to Portlanders.

And others took notice. Portland's affordable livability has attracted waves of artists and progressives intent on making the world a better place. They continue to build upon the city's history of community spirit and sense of possibility—after all, this was a town where neighbors could tear down a freeway! Where citizens could stop a highway and install a light rail instead! Where a four-thousand-acre forest was left standing in the middle of the city! And, yes, a place where food carts would be allowed to take over vacant lots throughout town.

Often people move here first and find a job later. As Trey Corkern, a food cart owner and recent transplant to Portland observes, "People want to live here and will do what it takes to live here." Newcomers to Portland are seeking the good life—they aren't out to strike it rich. In fact, in his book Carl Abbott goes so far as to say that Portland has a strong ethic of "conspicuous underconsumption." This characteristic was not lost on Matt Gross, the *New York Times'* Frugal Traveler, on a visit to Portland in 2009. He observed that Portland has "…a general indifference to wealth. In its place was a dedication to the things that really matter: hearty food and drink, cultural pursuits both high and low, days in the outdoors and evenings out with friends. It's the good life, and in Portland it still comes cheap." It only makes sense that Portlanders would welcome the budget-oriented, family-friendly, casual-spirited food cart industry with open arms. It helps that Portlanders love to support quirkiness and independence in a variety of ways. Locals are

quite proud of the city's unusually eclectic list of superlatives: one of the most bicycle-friendly cities in the country, the highest number of breweries per capita in the country, the smallest park in the world (Mill Ends Park), the largest urban chicken population in the United States, the highest number of strip clubs per capita in the country, and beloved Powell's—the country's largest independent bookstore. They celebrate independence of spirit in its many forms and go out of their way to support craft over mass production. Given the option, most Portlanders will choose local, independent, and eccentric over corporate and predictable.

Cultural openness, creative spirit, affordability, quality of life—these are all key ingredients that have made Portland a successful entrepreneurial experiment, according to Charles Heying, a Portland State University professor and author of *Brew to Bikes*:

Portland's Artisan Economy. It's the kind of place where food carts can thrive. Kevin Cavenaugh's experience as a Loeb Fellow at Harvard supports this sentiment. "When I was back east for a year, everyone was really dismissive of new ideas," says Kevin. "'But wait!' I would tell them, 'I'm talking about something that's already happening, something that's been proven, but on a tiny scale.' Somehow Portland, its small scale and its openness to ideas, makes it a great laboratory for food carts... and other entrepreneurial ventures for that matter."

One aspect of this openness is a history of collaboration and information sharing. The venture-capital model—invent, invest, sell, and make a killing—doesn't resonate here. This collaborative spirit is reflected down to the level of the carts. "Vendors are generally helpful to each other," says Rick Zeidman of Northwest Mobile Kitchens, a builder of custom food carts. "They are very open to letting others take a look inside and see how it's done. They think, 'The pie is big enough.'" Ray Koernig, from the Curbside Grill in Sellwood, appreciated that aspect of cart culture immediately. "What I like about the carts is how open everyone is," says Ray. "Most carts try to complement each other's offerings, not compete."

By and large, cart owners tend to reflect the traits of many Portlanders. According to the *Food Cartology* study, "many vendors enter the food cart business…because of their desire for independence, flexibility, and as a stepping-stone for opening their own restaurants." In fact, they found that 68 percent of vendors named independence as their *first* priority, even over making profits.

Artisanal, quirky, independent, and an exceptionally good value, the food carts are in many ways the perfect symbol of what Portland is all about. They bring the local community together with the lure of good food, and the pod system has enabled vendors to create a strong cooperative ethic among themselves. It's fair to say that the food carts both stem from Portland's famed livability and contribute to it, forming another "virtuous cycle" of sorts.

THE ECONOMY

While food carts have long been a feature of Portland's food scene, their

numbers have exploded in recent years. From 2008 to 2009, the number of food carts increased 30 percent, and today their total number hovers around five hundred. Why the increase? All cultural and culinary aspects aside, the financial model is incredibly appealing, especially in a down economy. Compared to the investment of starting a new brick-and-mortar restaurant, the start-up costs for a food cart are quite manageable. The low barrier to entry makes it an attractive option for many, including immigrants with limited access to resources, culinary-school graduates with debt, and those recently laid off from their jobs.

Generally, early adopters of the food cart business model are recent immigrants. Although Portland's food cart scene isn't dominated by ethnic food, as it tends to be in other cities, immigrants nevertheless constitute a sizable percentage of street vendors. *Food Cartology* found that "over half of the food cart vendors surveyed outside the CBD [central business district] are Hispanic, whereas there is a greater mix of ethnicities (Hispanic, Caucasian, and Asian) within the CBD. In addition, more than half (51%) of the vendors surveyed were born outside of the US."

Food carts are popular with immigrants for several reasons. First, immigrants—particularly those with limited English—may find it more challenging to navigate the traditional job market; it seems easier to run their own show instead. Others find it a natural transition from work they did in their home country. The setup is remarkably similar: vending from carts located on the street, toting in water, using propane as cooking fuel. Jonath Colon of the Hispanic Metropolitan Chamber says immigrants

VENDORS OF TAQUERIA URUAPAN

Bartolo and Araceli moved to Portland from Santa Ana, California, to run this traditional Michoacano cart, owned by Araceli's younger brother. Araceli and Bartolo learned to cook from Araceli's sister, who owns a number of Mexican restaurants in town. They moved to the Cully neighborhood to be close to the cart and have found over the past three years that many people from Michoacán live close by. As a result, their cart has become a gathering place where those missing the flavors of home can come and eat traditional foods like *lengua* (tongue) and *cabeza* (head)—as well as fare more familiar to Americans, such as carne asada, carnitas, and vegetarian tacos. But it's more than just Mexican neighbors who frequent the cart—people come from all over Portland to eat the couples traditionally prepared cuisine. Bartolo and Araceli would love to own their own cart or even open their own restaurant someday, but for the time being, are satisfied with running Taqueria Uruapan.

arriving to the United States with big dreams are sometimes disappointed to discover that their best work opportunity is to open a food cart. However, after a couple of months of operation, they see that it's an honest and profitable way to make a living and their disappointment fades. For many immigrants, food cart ventures are the stepping stone to owning their own restaurants.

In a similar vein, when Supakjanat "Pbong" Brunjongaksorn married Kris Haefker

and moved to Oregon, she started a Thai food cart—in the front yard of their home. Kris explained that opening a cart at their home was the obvious thing for his wife to do. "Pbong doesn't like to drive, and the concept of getting in your car to go to work is a foreign concept to her. It's natural to have your business at home."

When the economy turned, a new wave of vendors joined the food cart scene. "A lot

of [food cart owners] are creative, hard-working, young individuals," said Roger Goldingay, developer of the Mississippi Marketplace in North Portland, in an interview in *Oregon Business*. "They have a little cash in a down economy and they're creating their own jobs." These new-school vendors include those recently laid off from work, culinary-school graduates, and people from the restaurant industry who are fed up with the rigors and hierarchy of the restaurant world. Trey Corkern was almost forty and stuck in a rut working at local restaurants for $10 an hour, but the prospect of opening his own restaurant wasn't attractive or financially viable. So he bought a food cart at the SW Fifth and Oak location and has found solid footing at The Swamp Shack. "Food carts are a cook's dream," Trey concluded.

Of course, part of a carts' appeal is the low overhead. Basic costs for operating a food cart include the purchase or lease of a cart, any cart improvements (like signage), the rental of a space, the cooking equipment, and the food costs. If a cart is able to hire staff, then labor costs must be factored into the equation as well. Of course, costs can vary tremendously depending on how vendors source their food. Vendors buying meat from Cash and Carry, a discount cororate grocer, will have lower food costs than those who buy from Tails and Trotters, a locally sourced meat supplier. But what they aren't paying for—waitstaff, tables and linens, brick-and-mortar rents—is what keeps the costs at a level well below a typical restaurant.

Used food carts can be bought online for as little as $2,000, although a cart at that price will likely require renovation work.

If a vendor wants to start from scratch, with a solid structure that meets health code, including a hot-water tank, cold-water storage, and gray-water storage, it will cost about $15,000, according to Bryan Johnson of Innovision Homes, who builds custom food carts. Depending on how elaborate the design—or how expensive the equipment—a custom cart can cost up to $30,000 or more. Vendors who don't have the money up-front to purchase a cart sometimes have the option to lease a cart along with the space. So in addition to paying the typical $300–600 per month for the space, they'd pay about $500 per month for the cart.

While vendors are reluctant to release specific information about their profits, many of them are clearly managing to get by. According to the PSU Food Cartology study, most vendors (in stationary mobile units) are making between $30,000 and $50,000 a year. Although vendors will readily admit that the food cart business is certainly not the ticket to the easy life—these are lean operations that involve long hours and narrow margins—many have nevertheless found a measure of stability and satisfaction with this way of life.

Amanda Rhoads

OWNER OF SCOOP

Ice cream was always the honored dessert in Amanda Rhoads's house when she was growing up. As she says, "My parents were addicted. We [even] had several different ice cream makers on hand should the mood strike." She had never considered making ice cream professionally, though, until she got laid off in 2009 from her position as a long-range planner for the City of Portland. As she debated her options, she realized she wanted not just another job, but a lifestyle change. She wanted to find work that she could do in the evenings and on weekends so that she could spend more time with her young son, Oscar. She had always felt that Portland was missing ice cream—for a city that can support two dozen chocolatiers, how can there not be more independent, small-batch ice cream shops? After several months of research and planning, she landed at Refuel North Station with her rehabbed 1963 mini step van. She's already established a loyal following and loves the summer months, when she can experiment with fresh local produce as it comes into season. It's hard for Amanda to pick a favorite among her organic ice cream creations, but salted caramel, triple-threat ginger, avocado, and oatmeal and brown sugar top the list.

delicious, hand—crafted organic ice c
Scoop
organic ice cream

Part Three

HOW FOOD CARTS ARE CHANGING THE URBAN LANDSCAPE

The explosive growth of food carts runs counter to the usual trend in urban regeneration. Typically when a city center becomes a place where middle- and upper-middle-class people want to spend time, the architectural code of conduct becomes more formal, more carefully constructed. Food carts, with their budget-driven, ad hoc designs, take a city in the opposite direction.

– Philip Langdon, *New Urban News*

ood carts have transformed Portland's landscape, literally and figuratively, but what will happen next? How will this phenomenon continue to evolve? And how will the carts continue to push the boundaries of urban life? The vendors themselves are exploring new business models, including different forms of food cart operations, ownership of multiple carts, and even brick-and-mortar restaurants. But Portland food carts are doing more than pushing beyond traditional concepts of design and food. They are challenging ideas about the scale at which development can occur, illustrating how local businesses can have a ripple effect through the economy, and even shining a spotlight on what sustainable economic development really means and how it is financed. As a result of the food cart explosion, Portland may very well be on the leading edge of a massive trend toward localization—a concept that has enjoyed many years of theoretical support, and is finally evolving into a proven economic development force.

THE GREAT DEBATE: CARTS VS. RESTAURANTS

Food cart owners are continually asked whether their carts are a stepping stone to a restaurant or a satisfying end unto themselves. It's a good question. Indeed many vendors do view their food cart as a strategic step toward their end goal of opening a restaurant, and it's a clever strategy. Beginning with a food cart allows owners to do two key things before investing in a full-blown restaurant: test their concept with relatively low overhead, and build customer loyalty.

Addy Bittner knew she eventually wanted to open a neighborhood café, but started with a cart, "because I knew the start-up costs would be a lot lower than jumping into opening an actual storefront. It was a way of easing into being in business without too much financial risk." The café is still her end goal, and her investment in the cart will help her get there. Addy isn't alone in her hope to make it into bricks and mortar. Matt Breslow from the Grilled Cheese Grill intends to go brick-and-mortar within five years. By then, he figures he'll have a sizable following and an established reputation that make

the prospect of a permanent location much less risky. However, vendors often find the financial costs to be a barrier, since the outlay for opening a storefront restaurant is in another league entirely. Even successful food carts have had difficulty making the transition, although several carts—No Fish! Go Fish!, Koi Fusion, The Whole Bowl, and Taqueria los Gorditos, for example—have proven that it's possible.

Other vendors are content to stick with the cart business model, though their rationale varies. For some, the main

appeal is the autonomy it allows them; they get to be in charge without the burden of too many employees. Kirsten Jensen, for instance, realized—after two different stints working in restaurants—that she never wanted to work for someone else again. Others like the fact that a cart allows them to dedicate themselves to the perfection of a single dish: Nong Poonsukwattana has made a name for herself with her Khao Man Gai, the only dish on her menu. While that may sound limiting, she's got long lines and a stellar reputation for that one offering.

It's not always a case of either/or. Some vendors own multiple carts (Zona Rosa, for instance, has about six carts scattered across the city), while others own both a cart and restaurant. After the success of Potato Champion at Cartopia, Mike McKinnon opened a second food cart called Spudnik that roves around town, supplying the populace with Belgian fries. Andrea Spella, of the well-loved Spella's Caffe, always intended to open a café, but got sidetracked

The Beef on Competition

Although most locals are singing the praises of food carts these days, there are, to be fair, a few detractors. Restaurateurs in particular have mixed feelings about these interlopers, who see the carts as direct competition with the unfair advantages of lower costs and fewer regulatory hoops to jump through. While a few restaurants are going with the "If you can't beat 'em, join 'em" model and trying to get in on the cart action themselves (Burgerville, a local fast food chain, has its own truck—dubbed Nomad—in order to broaden its reach to the cart audience), restaurant owners are generally the least enthusiastic of neighborhood business owners.

What are they grumbling about exactly? Well, they complain that the stationary mobile carts aren't paying system development charges (SDCs), which are fees that help finance and maintain the development of the city's infrastructure. (To be fair, food carts aren't actually the beneficiaries of much infrastructure, since they often tote in their own water and manage their own wastewater.) Furthermore, restaurants enjoy all sorts of advantages that carts don't—more space, more varied offerings, shelter, longer leases, and more profit potential. Yes, carts may be legitimate competition in terms of their offerings, but given that carts are at the mercy of all sorts of other forces—weather and limited space, to name just two variables—it's a bit of a stretch to claim they actually have an unfair competitive *advantage*.

It's interesting to note that this very argument has raged along the same lines around the world. Irene Tinker, a former University of California Berkeley professor who now

lives in Portland, has studied street food internationally. The complaint by established businesses, Tinker explains, is nearly universal in the world of street vending. But try as they might, the authorities can't eradicate street food. The demand is too high. As Tinker notes, "food carts never disappear. They just evolve." Urbanist William Whyte is more pointed: "Merchants will keep up the fight against vendors—but victory will continue to be elusive….Over time you cannot enforce a law that is against something people like….Authority is being refuted by the marketplace. The vendors are providing what the established order is not."

when he saw the cart for sale. Realizing that the cart would be an easier way to get his fledgling business up and running, he bought the cart, established a loyal following, and then went on to lease a brick-and-mortar space nearby. And in a restaurant-to-cart reversal, the owners of Violetta Restaurant, faced with delays in opening their brick-and-mortar location, began instead with a cart, ETTA, to serve gourmet fare in Director Park downtown.

Carts are not just a good option for those with limited resources or when the economy is down; carts can be viewed as a critical part of the culinary continuum. They stand on their own as a legitimate business model or can be married to a larger operation. And although restaurants occasionally grumble about food carts taking away their business or about their unfair competitive advantage, savvy entrepreneurs recognize that restaurants and food carts largely operate within different markets, and that having a food cart in addition to a restaurant is a good way to diversify. Restaurants and food carts ultimately complement, rather than compete with, each other, with each model serving different needs within the community and enriching the culinary and urban landscape in its own way.

THE NEW POD MODEL

Noting the carts' flexibility, quick start-up time, and low overhead, business developers and investors are finding that food carts are an excellent way to generate income on stalled development parcels or other sites that are hard to develop. Up until recently, cart development has tended to be organic in nature, with carts sprouting like wildflowers on vacant parcels. However, local business developers are currently testing new models of small-scale development that use food carts as the main draw. For the first time, developers are actually *encouraging* food carts to take root on their sites, and enticing them with a variety of amenities.

Business owner Roger Goldingay was about to start construction on a condo development on North Mississippi Avenue when the economy tanked and left him with a lot, but no buyers. Determined not to leave the lot empty, Goldingay was one of the first developers to envision the possibilities of a planned food cart pod. Although downtown parking-lot owners had been renting spaces out to carts for years, no one had intentionally developed a pod until Roger's Mississippi Marketplace. Roger renovated an old building on the edge of the lot into Prost, a German-style pub, then used the adjoining surface parking lot as a paved pedestrian plaza. He posted a request for cart proposals, selected about a dozen, and watched as they opened up for business. It was a good solution for everyone: he's making money off the lot, supporting small businesses, and providing the neighborhood with an amenity—all in all, not a bad deal.

Now that there's a successful model in place, others are getting in on the act. Eric

Cress and Neeley Wells of Urban Development Partners developed Good Food Here, a pod that will consist of eighteen to twenty-two carts at SE Forty-Third Avenue and Belmont Street. When they were given the option for this site, which had been a surface parking lot for thirty years, they weren't ready to take on another building project. They were trying to figure out what to do with the site when one of the partners walked in with a falafel from his favorite cart and said, "Let's do food carts!" Aside from the developers' love of good ethnic food, food carts were a logical fit for Urban Development Partners. "They're flexible and fast," says Neeley. "We can produce some income and effectively engage the community at the same time." Neeley's point about engaging the community

is important. Planned pods create more pleasant spaces, luring both vendors and customers with lots of appealing extras: more permanent infrastructure support facilities, shared covered eating space, lighting, restrooms, ATMs, signage, and utilities. Although the carts themselves still express plenty of personality, the overall effect is a bit more orderly, tidy, and cohesive.

Bernie Franceschi, a loyal cart customer, likes what is happening in local neighborhoods. "I like to eat in attractive surroundings," he said. "It doesn't need to be hoity-toity attractive. But food cart pods need to evolve into built spaces, not just a collection of carts." And that is precisely what is happening. "The evolution of the

Portland food cart will be wonderful to watch," said Kevin Cavenaugh. "Soon, I think, you'll see better seating options, more expansive hours of operation, and more care in designing the common shared spaces around the cart clusters."

Given the success of places like Mississippi Marketplace, it seems that everyone suddenly wants to fill every vacant lot with a food cart village. But it's critical for developers to consider location before jumping on the bandwagon, as food carts are not the quick fix for every vacant parcel of land. What works in areas with heavy pedestrian traffic and an absence of other food services is less apt to succeed farther off the grid. Jonath Colon of the Hispanic Metropolitan Chamber described one client who wanted to put a cart, "two blocks away from any retail traffic and in a noisy location. There was

nothing desirable about the site." He ultimately discouraged this would-be cart owner from launching his business in such a poor location.

With vacant parcels across the city sprouting food carts and the new trend in purpose-built pods, concerns of market saturation are another reason developers need to be strategic about location. Jason King, a landscape architect who worked with Urban Development Partners on Good Food Here, explored the demand for food carts in that neighborhood. "When we created a map of food cart locations across the city, there was a big hole at the Forty-Third and Belmont site," he said. Since there is little in the way of food cart competition and the area generally lacks in services for residents living along upper Belmont Street, a food cart pod has a good chance of success here. Jason also suspects that loner carts might abandon their solitary spots and join an already established pod or create their own cluster to draw more foot traffic and increase business.

The pod concept is not only an interesting place-making phenomenon, but actually integral to the business model and survival of many of these street vendors. "Critical mass is important," says Brett Burmeister. "It's best for cart owners to focus on one or two things and do it well. The other carts provide the other menu options, the diversity for

people to choose from." In fact, a visit to a food cart pod usually begins with a stroll up and down the sidewalk to check out the menus and the lines. Customers tired of waiting for a popular cart—an anchor tenant, one might say—might defect to another cart with a shorter line. In this way, carts passively support each other.

Food carts have already demonstrated that they are adaptable, evolving to meet culinary tastes, economic trends, and neighborhood character. If current trends are any indication,

they are likely to become even better looking, more integrated into the community, and a more permanent feature of the urban landscape. "Rather than some kind of novelty or fad, I certainly hope the food cart phenomenon is one of many defining elements of a new urban culture," says Bernie Franceschi. As we will see in the next section, there are strong indications that food carts could be part of a new way to build the city.

URBANISM & LOCALISM:
A RETURN TO THE STREET

In recent years, Portland has become famous as a model metropolis, one that has proven that increasing density and urbanity can make a city more livable and attractive. As other cities see a resurgence in popularity they're working fast to catch up and create

the appealing neighborhoods and pedestrian-friendly streets that urban dwellers desire. This scale of living—the scale of the pedestrian—supports a different kind of retail than the car-focused scale of the suburbs. Food carts, as microenterprises supported by foot traffic, are the perfect model for this new trend toward urbanism. Bernie Franceschi is looking forward to this shift. "There are many points of entrance into building a physical environment that will result in a much more sustainable, beautiful, and human-scale interpersonal polis," says Bernie. "Food carts are certainly one important component."

Alma Flores, a city planner in Portland's Bureau of Planning and Sustainability, is a strong advocate for food carts and their role in supporting urban vitality and the local economy. "Not every parcel in the city is ready for development," Alma says. She explains that food carts are a good interim development measure for those lots that have been slow to develop. Marcy McInelly of SERA Architects agrees that food carts are a logical choice for undeveloped property. "No building could go on one of these parking lots that would make financial sense. Even before the economy tanked, development on many of these lots wasn't viable." Architect Joseph Readdy adds that there are often complications with developing surface lots, particularly downtown. The lots might be tied to leases with other buildings to offer parking to those buildings' tenants. Furthermore, if a site is located in a historic district, it might be easier and more profitable to keep

it as a parking lot than to construct a new building that adheres to the strict codes that regulate historic districts.

Generally, city planners aren't fond of surface parking lots, food cart populated or not, because they would rather see a mixed-use building that meets their urban design objectives. However, food carts mitigate the urban eyesore while filling an important economic niche—much like a pioneer species occupying a place in an evolving ecosystem. Indeed, food carts are critical economic pathways, particularly for immigrant populations, and if the market can't support new condos and twenty-thousand-square-foot chunks of ground-floor retail, why not let food carts prosper?

But beyond that, Alma Flores believes food carts are showing developers a different model for urban development and retail space: "This is not just a planning issue," says Alma, "this is development, finance, economics." In her article "Food Carts as Retail Real Estate," published in the PSU Center for Real Estate's *Quarterly & Urban Development Journal*, April Chastain estimates that food carts in the city of Portland "collectively occupy between 48,000 SF and 92,000 SF of retail space and pay between $2 million and $5 million per year in rent." She observes that the Alder pod alone, which has roughly "29 food carts wrapping around five faces of the two parking lot blocks," collectively represents 15,000 square feet of retail space. As this pod demonstrates, developers theoretically *could* lease out a 15,000- or 20,000-square-foot retail space—if they were just willing to divide into food cart–sized chunks.

Micro-retail may in fact be a good transition to brick-and-mortar space for food cart owners. These mini spaces are carved out of a wall in a building and typically serve deli food or coffee directly to customers lined up on the sidewalk. According to Marcy McInelly, micro-retail spaces were initially created to enliven blank facades in Portland's downtown storefronts in the 1980s. A few new micro-retail spaces have opened up recently, including an alcove at Macy's for Elephant's Deli and a niche in the wall on NE Alberta Street for Parkers Waffles.

Kevin Cavenaugh has been interested in micro-retail for several years. "Micro-retail isn't new," Kevin explains. "It's something that happens in places where land is really expensive—like Manhattan or Toyko—but they don't call it that." Three years ago, understanding that people want places with low overhead, Kevin was developing a building with small spaces—"enough for a desk and a photocopier"—and had several tenants lined up, including an artist, an architect, and a florist. But then the economy went south and he couldn't find funding. Today, he's developing another space, and this time all his tenants are food purveyors. "There is an ocean between a food cart and a restaurant," says Kevin. "I want to swim in that ocean."

Having observed the possible over-saturation of food carts in Portland and their somewhat precarious seasonal existence, Kevin is betting that many food cart owners are ready to step up to a permanent space with greater shelter from the elements, without having to invest in a full-blown restaurant. "We've seen the bottom of the entry to the restaurant world and what people are willing to accept," he says. "So now we

should be talking about a slightly more sophisticated design and a little bigger space." His units range from 225 square feet to 375 square feet and will rent out for between $690 and $990 a month. The spaces will share storage, refrigeration, and dishwashing equipment. Kevin noted that payroll is the biggest expense facing restaurant owners, and the second is rent. "If I can cut rent down by 80 percent, and then cut payroll by 80 percent, you only need to sell thirty Whiffie's pies a day to make it." Who knows. It could very well be the start of a whole new trend.

With cart owners having proved the success of the small, lean business model, developers are beginning to see the merits of carving micro-retail out of the most unlikely spaces—even just the narrowest of blank walls. And everyone wins: the vendor enjoys lower overhead than in a big space, the developer gets a little extra money, and the customer has more amenities to choose from.

The scale of these small enterprises makes perfect sense if we are willing to look at them within the framework of a different economy and financial system moving forward. In addition to being a food cart supporter, Bernie Franceschi is also a financial planner. "The economy is not going back to the way it was—it was built on a deck of cards," says Bernie. "People will become more value-conscious—it will be a permanent thing, something that will mark people," which means that people will continue to eat at food carts because of their value and quality. "Economizing will become a discovery," theorizes Bernie. "It's an opportunity for the non-franchised, one-of-a-kind business."

FINANCING THE SHIFT

Interestingly, new infrastructure is also developing to encourage and support the micro-entrepreneur—further evidence that micro-retail is gaining traction as a viable economic model. Mercy Corps is offering micro-loans to help independent entrepreneurs establish themselves in these micro-spaces. Mercy Corps began funding food carts in 2002 and is now funding up to fifteen a year. The average loan size is $13,000, although recent requests have been trending upward toward $20,000. Like popular micro-lending programs in developing countries, these micro-loans are filling an important economic niche for those with little access to other resources. They are successful, too. Most of the food cart cash-flow projections show carts breaking even within the first three to six months and having a positive cash flow by the end of their first year.

Many of the vendors at the Mississippi Marketplace received financial support from Albina Opportunities Corporation, a nonprofit that caters specifically to Portland's underserved small businesses and distressed neighborhoods. Their aim is to create jobs, particularly for small minority- or women-owned businesses, by connecting these businesses to lenders. Terry Brandt, the executive director of Albina Opportunities Corporation, finds that food carts are a good investment: "They are simple, you get immediate financial feedback (you've got it or you don't), they pay living-wage rates, provide business opportunities with a low capital investment, add significantly to our community culture, and are just plain fun."

Again, the scale of food carts is a critical part of their economic success: "As a small-

business promoter, I like to think in terms of very human-scale operations that a lot of us can identify with and actually see ourselves doing," says Terry. "Something requiring a small capital investment, little long-term commitment to a lease, a simple break-even profitability, and a pride of ownership. At the end of the day, this small-scale approach, if done in every sector of our economy, could represent the tail that wags the dog."

Informal micro-loans are another way of bridging the financing gap, and illustrate the power of community. When Andrea Spella decided to expand to his brick-and-mortar

location, he asked some of his most loyal customers if they would be interested in investing. Bernie Franceshi chose to invest, not only as a customer-turned-friend of Andrea, but also because of his desire to "build a more localized, independent, and interdependent economy." He observes, "communities grow through localized economies," and this was his chance to practice what he preaches. But the real point here is that individuals— loyal customers who have had a chance to observe the micro-retail phenomenon in practice—have enough faith in the formula to put their own money into it.

RELATED INDUSTRIES

The rapidly growing local food cart industry has also begun to generate its own demands, fueling further economic growth in satellite industries. One example is the increased demand for commissary kitchens, which was great enough that Mike McKinnon from Potato Champion decided to open his own commissary kitchen. Today he earns extra income from that kitchen, which caters to other food cart owners who require a place to prepare food for the day. As a side business, Francisco Castenda, who owns Tito's Burritos at SW Tenth and Alder, offers a gray-water disposal service to food carts.

Building custom food carts is another side industry. Bryan Johnson of Innovision Homes found that building food carts was a timely complement to the downturn in the home-remodeling industry. He initially built a cart to help his friend Jeremy, the owner of the Portland Soup Company, but once he was done, Bryan began getting calls from other interested parties. To date, he's built three carts—including Ruby Dragon—and has two more in the works.

When architect Rich Zeidman and chef Jason Britsas first met, they had plans to open their own food cart. However, as they began shopping for carts and discovered they'd likely need to have one shipped from Florida or California, they realized a local market opportunity existed to build custom carts. As Northwest Mobile Kitchens, LLC, they assist cart owners with the specifications and design of their carts and have built carts for Big-Ass Sandwiches and Garden State, among others.

Indeed, if the cart form itself is a successful enterprise, why should it be limited to

selling food? Until recently, carts have been dominated by food vendors, but there are signs that other businesses are jumping on the bandwagon. For example, a truck downtown on SW Third Avenue carries cigarettes and magazines. One of Jonath Colon's clients is converting a truck into a mobile hair salon and is planning to visit assisted-living facilities

and other places that lack good access to services. In some cases, non-food goods or services such as bike repair, doggie day care, a clothing boutique, and even dry-cleaning businesses are beginning to share space with food carts. The eclectic assortment of carts and businesses at North Fremont Street and Vancouver Avenue is one such pod: it features three food carts, a shoe-repair shop, and a dry-cleaners on an abandoned gas-station site that is in development limbo.

Northwest Mobile Kitchens is interested in this mixed-use application of the carts. Rich Zeidman calls them mobile merchants. "Let's put a shoemaker or a keymaker in there," says Rich. "Those small guys can't afford retail rents." Rich wants these smaller businesses to have better success, and one way to achieve that is to offer customers a more varied mix of retail. One new example of this trend is a collection of carts that have popped up on a vacant lot at the corner of NE Martin Luther King Jr. Boulevard and Jarrett

Street. The vendors offer an assortment of goods and services from their carts—records, barbecue, and a barber—and the space feels more like a flea market in spirit than a food court.

CONCLUSION

Portland is projected to grow in population, and its commitment to livability means growing up, not out. As the city becomes denser, walking is likely to become an increasingly appealing alternative to driving, and it's reasonable to think that the number of carts offering a greater variety of goods and services will continue to increase. In fact, in its regulatory guidebook for carts in the public right-of-way, the City of Portland specifically indicates that carts are appropriate for fresh-cut flowers, shoe shines, umbrellas, and,

oddly, inflated balloons. The hope is that this list will expand to include more amenities and goods.

The popularity of the pint-sized cart is very clearly demonstrating that bigger isn't always better. Coinciding with a return to localism and urbanism, food carts are well positioned to be the new food-business model of choice for vendors, developers, and customers alike. At the same time, they are the pioneers, pushing the boundaries of the traditional urban landscape, encouraging us all to think more creatively about our local economies and the role we want our city streets to play.

Portland's love affair with food carts isn't likely to end anytime soon, although perhaps the relationship will evolve into something more sophisticated and more permanent. But we wouldn't want to lose the spontaneity, the creativity, the delicacy, and the charm that brought them together in the first place. After all, food carts are very much what Portlanders love about Portland: local, independent, eclectic, down-to-earth, and delicious.

Part Four

THE GUIDE

Documenting the whereabouts of the 500-plus food carts in Portland is a daunting, if not impossible, task. With dozens of pods across the city and loner carts popping up in lots between buildings like dandelions, tracking and reviewing food carts could be a full-time job. We've opted instead to highlight the city's most popular and distinctive food cart pods, showcasing vendor and architectural highlights as well as great food, of course.

For the most current details on carts, their whereabouts, hours of operation, and other helpful stats, visit FoodCartsPortland.com.

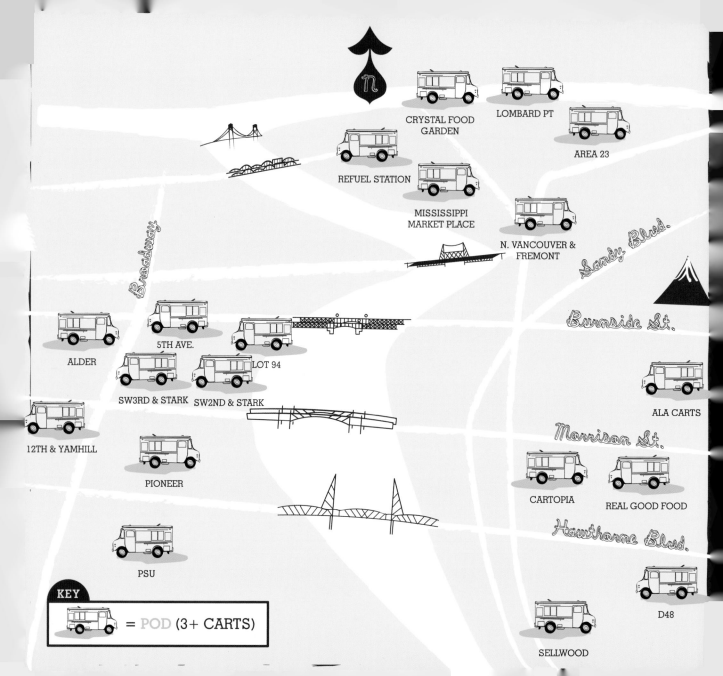

CRYSTAL FOOD GARDEN

LOMBARD PT

AREA 23

REFUEL STATION

MISSISSIPPI MARKET PLACE

N. VANCOUVER & FREMONT

Sandy Blvd.

Burnside St.

Broadway

ALDER

5TH AVE.

LOT 94

SW3RD & STARK

SW2ND & STARK

ALA CARTS

12TH & YAMHILL

PIONEER

Morrison St.

CARTOPIA

REAL GOOD FOOD

Hawthorne Blvd.

PSU

D48

SELLWOOD

KEY

= POD (3+ CARTS)

DISTRICT: SOUTHWEST

SW TWELFTH AVE AND YAMHILL STREET

Location:

SW Twelfth Avenue and Yamhill Street

Description:

Although this pod is small—it consists of only three carts—it's worth checking out for the noteworthy Indian food. India Chaat House has been at this spot for over ten years, serving lunchtime specials and dinner to customers who can enjoy their meal under a covered seating area. A few years ago the couple running the Chaat House divorced; the wife opened a second Indian cart, the Bombay Chaat House, right next door. Last year a Mexican cart opened, rounding out the pod.

Best Time of Day:

Weekday lunch and dinner

Types of Food:

Indian, Mexican

Vendor Profile

SHELLY SORENSON

Honkin' Huge Burritos

Shelly Sorenson operates Honkin' Huge Burritos out of a pushcart in Pioneer Square. With great pride and a well-earned sense of accomplishment, Shelly beams that she was "the first food cart in Portland." Eighteen years ago, Shelly was looking for a change in her life. "I found myself in a career that I just didn't like. I wanted to get out of the office and live, and I wanted to be passionate about what I was doing." She wanted to be engaged with work that better supported her values. On a trip to New Orleans she realized that a food cart would provide her with a livelihood that would support her vegetarian lifestyle and bring some cheer to downtown office workers. More than 250,000 burritos later, she's still a die-hard fan of the cart lifestyle. "I love it. I do it every day. It's not work—it's what I love to do. That's the Zen of it. I watch the world go by from this one spot."

SOUTHWEST

ALDER & NINTH

Location:
Alder Street at SW Ninth & Tenth Avenues

Description:
This active pod is popular with the lunchtime office crowd, thanks to the diversity and quality of the food on offer. This pod was originally at Ninth and Alder but has expanded across to Tenth Avenue to create a multi-block food cart scene with some of the best food in the city.

Best Time of Day:
Weekday lunchtime and early dinner

Types of Food:
Mediterranean, Thai, Turkish, Mexican, Chinese, German, espresso, Korean, sandwiches, BBQ, Vietnamese, Bosnian, frozen yogurt, crepes, soup, vegetarian, Peruvian, rice-and-bean bowls, fish-and-chips

Frying Scotsman

Alder Pod: SW Ninth and Alder

The owner of the Frying Scotsman, James, was born in Scotland and traveled the world cooking. He met a girl from Portland, married her, and moved here. He couldn't find work, so he opened a "chip shop," because every town needs some proper British fish-and-chips. Today, he makes a living selling cod, haddock, halibut, red snapper, and mahi mahi, all lightly battered with a recipe from grandma, fried to order, and butter-soft. They're served with big, chunky potatoes, malt vinegar, and HP Sauce, a brown fruit-and-spice sauce that sounds like it's the A1 of the UK, only better. And, of course, all this comes with a thick accent and dry humor.

REID BARRETT & JULIA FILIP

The Dump Truck

Julia and Reid were both living and working in Beijing (her: overseeing manufacturing for a sports apparel company, him: editor at a publishing company) when they met in 2007. Both were huge dumpling fans, but Julia had developed a special connection to a couple named Ma, who owned a dumpling restaurant near her house. Julia ate a lot of dumplings during those years, and she eventually became an expert dumpling maker herself.

When they left Beijing and came to Portland, Julia missed dumplings so much that she and Reid would often make them for dinner using a set of bamboo steamers they had brought back from China. Serendipitously, their friend Scott Simon, owner of the karaoke bar Voicebox, was looking for someone to supply dumplings for their menu. Julia spent the next year crafting unique dumpling and sauce creations. She expanded her repertoire well beyond classic Chinese dumplings, experimenting with delicious and ridiculous variations such as bacon-cheeseburger dumplings and apple-pie dumplings served with vanilla ice cream. By the end of that first year, the dumplings were selling so well that Julia and Reid decided to open a food cart, inspired by an Asian Station Café cart for sale (which sold a few types of dumplings). Although they didn't buy that cart, they became close to the owner, Mel, and learned about the food cart business from him. They eventually bought an old bakery truck, renovated it, and work the business together—Reid as front man and Julia as chef.

SOUTHWEST

PIONEER COURTHOUSE SQUARE

Location:
SW Sixth Avenue and Yamhill Street

Description:
Located in the heart of downtown, Pioneer Courthouse Square is affectionately known as "Portland's living room." Created in 1984, Pioneer Courthouse Square has had food pushcarts since the early days. One perk is on-site seating, and there's great people-watching from the steps. You'll find tourists, office workers, and shoppers all lining up here.

Best Time of Day:
Weekday lunchtime, all day Saturday

Types of Food:
Burritos, burgers, cheesesteaks

SW FIFTH AVENUE

Location:
SW Fifth Avenue between Stark and Oak Streets

Description:
One of the earliest pods in Portland and conveniently located near the heart of downtown, the Fifth and Stark pod serves an eclectic mix of hungry office workers, bike couriers, lawyers, and hipsters at lunchtime. The original cluster of about five carts has grown to over twenty, occupying almost the entire perimeter of the parking lot. Located on the transit mall, it has ample seating, and buskers provide entertainment on the street corners, making it one of downtown's more social and atmospheric pods.

Best Time of Day:
A couple of carts are open for breakfast, but this pod primarily serves the downtown weekday lunchtime crowd.

Types of Food:
Polish, Mediterranean, Vietnamese, Mexican, Czech, Cajun, sandwiches, cheesesteaks, Indian, Thai, hot dogs, Korean, vegetarian, soup and salad, burgers, BBQ, pizza

SOUTHWEST

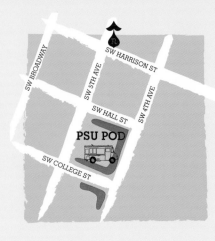

PSU POD

Location:
SW Fourth Avenue and Hall Street

Description:
This lively pod, located between the City of Portland offices and Portland State University, draws both bureaucrats and a diverse student population.

Best Time of Day:
Primarily weekday lunchtime, with a few carts open for breakfast

Types of Food:
Vegetarian, Thai, Korean, sandwiches, waffles, vegan, Lebanese, Mexican, Indian, soup

Buddha Bites

PSU POD: SW Fourth and Hall

As long as the folks at Buddha Bites keep wrapping scrambled eggs, bacon, cheese, and jam in a warm slice of naan, people will get in line. They also do a wonderfully filling meatloaf sandwich, and their veggie melt with peppers, onions, zucchini, cheese, and pesto sauce makes customers swoon. Whatever you do, don't miss one of their amazing fruit smoothies with almond milk or homemade kefir, a fermented milk drink high in antioxidants. Delicious, good for you, and good for the planet—everyone wins at Buddha Bites.

SCOTT SMITH

Bro-Dogs

Scott spent fifteen years in the mortgage banking industry and was vice president of a bank when the economy started taking a turn. He wasn't particularly happy there and didn't like the direction the industry was going. When his responsibilities were cut back, he decided it was time to try something new. After talking with his brother about the lack of good hot dogs in Portland, they decided to join forces and open a hot-dog stand together. One year into it, he's happy to say he loves it. "I can't imagine being one of the suits that comes by the cart—yeah, they're making more money than me…. But the happiness level? They always want to be me." The best part of having a cart is being his own boss. After managing 85 people in his former bank life, he also appreciates the simplicity of the cart. "None of this is that big a deal," Scott says. "If I forget onions, then I just put onions on."

Scott says that people ask him almost daily how to operate a cart and if they should go for it. "My response is always: 'Do it,'" says Scott. "No matter what their idea is." Scott was pleased to hear about Portland's top ranking for street food by CNN/*Budget Travel*: "That means I'm number one in the world—because I'm the number one vendor in Portland," Scott smiles, "And if Portland is number one in the world, then I'm the number one vendor in the world."

SOUTHWEST

SW THIRD AVENUE AND STARK STREET

Location:
SW Third Avenue and Stark Street

Description:
This pod along Third Avenue wraps around Stark Street, where it looks across at the neighboring pod at SW Second and Stark. With over twenty carts serving a variety of fare, this pod draws a big lunchtime crowd.

Best Time of Day:
Weekday lunchtime and late-night all week

Types of Food:
Mexican, Thai, Vietnamese, Egyptian, vegetarian, panini/sandwiches, pasta, Korean, smoothies, rice-and-bean bowls, sushi, Chinese, sausages, chili dogs/tamales, espresso, Celtic

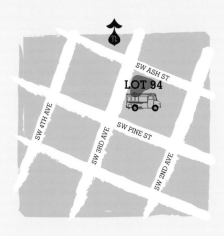

LOT 94

Location:
SW Third Avenue and Ash Street

Description:
A handful of carts cluster at this corner, drawing a downtown mix of business types, bike couriers, and hipsters with hearty lunch offerings. If you are lucky, you may see a band of feathered pirates eating Big-Ass Sandwiches.

Best Time of Day:
Weekday lunchtime, weekend breakfast, and late-night

Types of Food:
Burgers and sandwiches, Hawaiian, waffles

SOUTHWEST

SW SECOND AVENUE AND STARK STREET

Location:

SW Second Avenue and Stark Street

Description:

A single Mexican cart was operating on this lot until November 2009, when a host of others started rolling in. At press time, six carts regularly call this pod home, and a mobile cupcake truck visits on occasion. You won't be able to miss the bright-blue Sicilian cart, Joslyn's Ciao Chow—it was originally designed as a military cooking trailer, and stands head and shoulders above the rest on huge all-terrain wheels.

Best Time of Day:

Weekday lunchtime and late-night

Types of Food:

Cuban, Sicilian, Vietnamese, pork sandwiches, cupcakes

TREY CORKERN

The Swamp Shack

Trey spent the first twenty-five years of his life in Louisiana, about thirty miles outside of New Orleans. He moved to Portland a couple of years ago, bringing with him fifteen years of experience as a cook. Tired of working in restaurants where he had little opportunity to advance, he decided to open a food cart. He secured a location downtown and opened The Swamp Shack in May 2009. He likes the downtown location because he is surrounded by hungry office workers who "will always be here," and he wanted to work during the day rather than pulling the grueling nighttime hours demanded of a restaurant job. He also loves being his own boss and not managing employees. "It is a lot of work," he explains, "but in many ways it also keeps things simple." He is happy making a living doing something he enjoys, and even better, something he created himself: "I basically bought myself a job," says Trey.

NOTABLE LONER CARTS:
SOUTHWEST

NO FISH! GO FISH!

Location:
SW Fifth and Yamhill

Best Time of Day:
Weekday lunchtime

No Fish! Go Fish! has been in business in this spot half a block south of Pioneer Courthouse Square for thirteen years, serving up corn-fritter sandwiches in the shape of fish (they don't actually have any fish in them). You'll find a range of pollutant-free vegan, vegetarian, and meat options daily.

DISTRICT: NORTHWEST

In the densely developed Northwest neighborhood, there are few vacant lots for pods to camp on. Instead, carts fly solo here, operating on their own on or near commercial streets.

PBJ'S

Location:
NW Kearney Street and Twenty-Third Avenue

Best Time of Day:
Wednesday–Sunday lunch and dinner

Founded by Keena Tallman and Shane Chapman, PBJ's kicked off its cart career at 2010's Eat Mobile Fest under the Burnside Bridge. There, on their first day in business, PBJ's took home second-prize honors. "We moved to Portland to become entrepreneurs," Keena says. "We picked Portland for its beauty, amazing food and wine and beer, but most of all for the people."

After Keena's brother sampled several grilled peanut butter and jelly sandwiches at the Oregon Country Fair and raved about them, she made one for Shane, who loved it, too. They use local ingredients and sustainable products. As for the PBJ's themselves? They're almost too decadent to be true.

FOOD PROFILE

Koi Fusion

Roving Cart

There aren't many carts around town more colorful than this one, nor many with healthier food. In less than two years, Koi Fusion has quickly gained national notoriety as a leader in both artisan food carts and in the fast-growing genre of Korean fusion cooking. In fact, with a new stationary location and a full-time catering business already in its arsenal, Koi Fusion has almost completely outgrown its food truck status. But the spirit (and menu) of the place remains the same, and the unique approach—to combine Korean meats and marinades with Mexican styles and flavors—makes for an unusual, often alarmingly delicious meal. Koi Fusion's tacos are the best known and most beloved, and offer cheap, easy foodie exploration. Don't be surprised if Koi Fusion takes a place alongside Voodoo Doughnut and Stumptown Coffee as a must-have Portland staple.

DISTRICT: SOUTHEAST

ALA CARTS

Location:
SE 102nd Avenue and Stark Street

Description:
On the corner of a strip-mall parking lot at the busy intersection of 102nd and Stark, this mid-size pod provides much-needed alternatives in a neighborhood dominated by fast food. Next time you drive through outer Southeast Portland, be sure to stop by Happy Coffee at Ala Carts, where you can opt for one of the signature coffee drinks or, more fun, a root beer float. Take your food and drink to go, or sit down at the tables and chairs there.

Best Time of Day:
Early-morning coffee, lunch, and early dinner

Types of Food:
BBQ, Cuban, Mexican, Indian, Filipino, root beer floats and coffee, sausage dogs, stir-fry, rice bowls, noodles

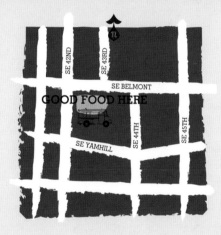

GOOD FOOD HERE

Location:
SE Belmont Street and Forty-Third Avenue

Description:
Good Food Here has a seating area with wooden picnic tables situated among trees and wooden planters. As of press time, it's supposedly going to be home to around twenty carts, promising a wide variety of culinary enticements.

Best Time of Day:
Weekday lunch and dinner, weekends all day

Types of Food:
French bistro, hot dogs/sausages, Mexican, Philly cheesesteak, garlic fries, Thai, Korean barbecue, meatballs, rice bowls, coffee, ice cream, Indian, Mediterranean, Greek, vegan and vegetarian options.

SOUTHEAST

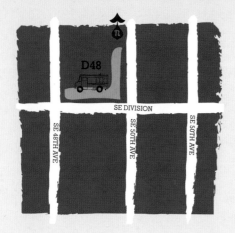

D48

Location:
SE Division Street and Forty-Eighth Avenue

Description:
On the site of the old A1 Bird Bath shop is a pod of about four carts. There are plans for the old garage to be turned into a coffee shop/bar.

Time of Day:
Daily lunch and early dinner

Types of Food:
Burgers, sandwiches, southern, Mexican, Korean barbecue

SELLWOOD POD

Location:
SE Thirteenth Avenue and Lexington Street

Description:
Located in the heart of the Sellwood neighborhood, this pod is densely packed with carts. Neighbors gather here in the early evenings, and bike parking and seating are provided. Don't miss Garden State, a Sellwood Pod veteran that moved half a block south of the pod along Thirteenth Avenue.

Best Time of Day:
Daily breakfast, lunch, and early dinner

Types of Food:
Italian ice, grilled sandwiches and salads, kids' menu, falafel, vegetarian options, coffee, Cuban, Thai, Mexican, Italian street food (half block south)

LAIZA CHAO
Bruce Lee's Kitchen

Laiza was born in Laos in 1968. After the American invasion of Vietnam, her family sought asylum in Thailand, where they remained for ten years before moving to the United States. In 2009 Laiza was laid off from her job assembling electrical equipment for Fiber SenSys. Not knowing what to do, she considered opening a food cart. Although she had never cooked professionally, she had grown up cooking for her family, and friends who'd sampled her cooking—particularly her boyfriend, the primary beneficiary—encouraged her to go into the food business. The small scale of the food cart model appealed to her, so she took the plunge and invested her small savings in a fully equipped cart in Sellwood. These days, she's working very hard, but also acknowledges that it's been a dream come true. She says, "When I sold my first order to someone who didn't know me and they said it was great, then I knew I had made the right decision."

SOUTHEAST

CARTOPIA

Location:
SE Twelfth Avenue and Hawthorne Street

Description:
Absolute mayhem on summer nights and after hours, this pod is not only a serious destination but a proper hangout with a sizable seating area. Don't be surprised when the band whose show you just saw bikes down here to eat after hours. Excellent people-watching.

Best Time of Day:
This late-night pod really starts hopping after the bars close. Prime time is around 1 a.m. nightly, although carts are open earlier in the evening and a few are even open for lunch.

Types of Food:
Pizza, crepes, vegan and vegetarian options, french fries, fried pies, Mexican, BBQ

NOTABLE LONER CARTS: SOUTHEAST

WOLF AND BEARS AND TREAT MACHINE

Location:
SE Twentieth Avenue and Morrison Street

Best Time of Day:
Wednesday–Saturday lunch through late dinner

Wolf and Bears' little trailer has its own covered seating—complete with a porch swing, should you feel the urge. They serve authentic Israeli food, such as the Sabich, a breakfast pita with grilled eggplant, cucumbers, onions, hard-boiled egg, and tahini. They also serve a falafel pita that is reputed to be the best in town. Their entire menu is vegetarian. Next door, a mini-cart called Treat Machine has opened up, serving 100 percent vegan tacos, fried plantains, and handmade tortillas.

SIP

Location:
SE Twenty-First Avenue and Tibbetts Street,
outside the People's Co-op

Best Time of Day:
Most days breakfast and lunch; Saturdays and Wednesday
evenings during the People's Co-op farmers' market are
especially hopping

When Sip founder Brian Heck first moved to Portland,
he got by thanks to the dumpster diving he did at New
Seasons and Trader Joe's, often leaving him with a bundle of fresh produce—more than he
could eat, in fact. "So I went to Goodwill and bought a $20 juicer," he explains, "and started
juicing it all." It wasn't long before he was hooked and "juicing every day." Soon after, Sip
was born. "It encompasses the best of both my worlds, my vegan sweet tooth and a love
for fresh healthy organic juice and smoothies," he says. Located outside one of Portland's
finest food co-ops, his cart turns the intersection from a grocery stop into a proper haven
for healthy, local, delectable food and drink.

FOOD PROFILE / DISTRICT: NORTH PORTLAND

Ruby Dragon

MISSISSIPPI MARKETPLACE: N. Mississippi and Skidmore

There aren't many carts around town more colorful than this one, nor many with healthier food. In fact, the cart and the food just about glow! You, too, will become a believer when you taste their quinoa pancakes, part of the "eternal morning" breakfast menu: flapjacks made with fresh-ground quinoa flour ("a complete protein") and hemp seeds, topped with real maple syrup, blueberries, and walnuts. Another favorite is The Abbot, an open-faced sandwich with curried tempeh on a bed of curried glazed cashews and "veganaise" on Dave's Killer Bread. A bouquet of yellow, orange, and gold, it's almost like a festival in your mouth. You just can't go wrong here. Whatever you choose, you'll feel like a healthier, happier person, and likely be back again within the week.

DISTRICT: NORTHEAST

AREA 23

Location:
NE Alberta Street and NE 23rd Avenue

Description:
Located on a gravel lot on the southeast corner of 23rd and Alberta, this pod has excellent food, proper seating, and great architecture. Solar panels, a flaming lotus sculpture (attached to one of the carts), and a beautiful streetcar named Inspire are only a few of the distinctive features of this pod. On the northwest corner of 23rd and Alberta, a beautifully restored double-decker bus has opened as the Bristol Café, serving sausages and sandwiches, also with adjacent outdoor seating.

Best Time of Day:
Weekday late lunch, dinner, all day weekends

Types of Food:
Smoothies and pie, waffles, tapas, Venezuelan, vegan and vegetarian options

MELISSA ORION
Inspire

Melissa Orion, a Portland native, mother, and artist, had been scouting around for her next collaborative project when she happened upon a post describing a vintage streetcar that was for sale. The wheels began to turn, and the next thing she knew, she and a cadre of eleven other performing artists were carefully packing the pieces of the streetcar onto a trailer to bring it back to Portland. With the help of some forty volunteers, she remodeled the interior into the inviting and inspiring place it is today. Orion joined forces with baker, chef, and raw-food enthusiast Alissa Martucci and came up with a healthy menu. Today, the cart carries a full range of pies, cookies, wraps, smoothies, juices, and much more, all living and full of the sun's inspiration. As she says, "The story of Inspire is just that, a story that inspires. Our time working to build her proved to be a lesson in the power of goals and community. I am so grateful for the opportunity to share her with the world."

FOOD PROFILE
Fuego Burritos
Several Locations

Most Portlanders know and love the city's touchstones of comfort food—mac and cheese at the Montage, the inimitable Voodoo Doughnut, and the poutine of Potato Champion. Ask any downtowner, though, and the burritos of Fuego will almost surely be at the top of their list. The formula is simple: black beans and rice, chicken (optional), cheese (optional), salsa, sour cream or yogurt (a surprise, but try it), and guacamole (which they inevitably run out of). It may sound straightforward, but when you try their prepared beans and their smoky, grilled chicken, you'll understand the care and attention that goes into these sublime creations. They may not be authentically Mexican, but Fuego's burritos are the perfect archetype of a Mission-style burrito—huge, fresh, and enormously satisfying.

FOOD PROFILE / DISTRICT: SOUTHEAST

Perierra Crêperie
Cartopia: SW Twelfth and Hawthorne

The wait can be long, but many customers agree that it's worth the wait. At Perierra Crêperie, you can choose from both sweet and savory crepes, and the list of ingredient options is long and enticing. Whether you're craving smoked salmon with cream cheese, arugula, and lemon, or just a simple lemon-and-sugar crepe, you're sure to find a flavor combination to your liking. In fact, that long line may not be such a bad thing—you might need the time to decide just what your perfect medley will include.

Addy's Sandwich Bar

ALDER POD: SW Tenth and Alder

Tucked along the Tenth Avenue stretch of one of Portland's busiest midday cart pods, Addy's short menu and fresh selections are almost universally delicious. Addy's is, in many ways, what most Northwestern fare aspires to be—simple food, simply executed to be delicious. They're renowned for their duck confit sandwich with cranberry relish and shredded cabbage (which costs the same modest $6.50 as the rest of the menu), but every combination is expertly tailored. Most sandwiches contain only a few select ingredients, and this begets a beautiful clarity of flavor, to a degree that seems unlikely for what is, in the end, often a pretty straightforward sandwich. The city had virtually no dedicated sandwich shops just a few years ago, but Portland has since turned a corner to welcome a bevy of excellent shops—and none succeeds in such a simple, unpretentious, and richly satisfying way as Addy's Sandwich Bar.

Saucy's

REFUEL STATION: N. Killingsworth and Greeley

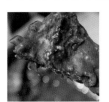

A relatively recent arrival, Saucy's specializes in backyard-BBQ fare—ribs, fish sandwiches, hot links, potato salad, and slaw. Their simple, straightforward, and highly affordable menu allows you to sample everything they've got for a mere $11. The standout is undoubtedly the $2 fish sandwich: Saucy's flash-fries savory white fish in a cornmeal crust, creating a rich, filling little sandwich with a fresh, bright flavor. Saucy's slaw is sure to start arguments—it's a sweet slaw, crisp and cold, with a hefty dose of pineapple, so consider yourself warned if you prefer yours savory. All told, in a region not known for its BBQ, Saucy's delivers the goods in a big way.

NORTHEAST

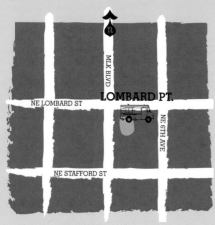

LOMBARD POINT

Location:
NE Martin Luther King, Jr. Avenue and Lombard Street

Description:
Formerly the home of a drive-through coffee cart, this site is currently home to four food carts, one of which sports the clever name of "Truck, Yeah!" But more carts are very likely on the way, as a dozen utility hook-ups are in place. At the moment, it draws a local lunchtime crowd, as well as late-night bar hoppers.

Best Time of Day:
Lunch and dinner

Types of Food:
BBQ, Mexican, cheeseburgers and steaks, Mediterranean

NOTABLE LONER CART: NORTHEAST

THE GRILLED CHEESE GRILL

Location:
NE Alberta Street and Eleventh Avenue

Best Time of Day:
Daily lunch to late afternoon, late-night weekends, unofficial dance party at midnight

Matt Breslow has taken the cart concept in a whole new direction. You'll understand what we mean when you see the lot where he's set up an Airstream camper kitchen and a seating area inside an old school bus. Complete with picnic tables and lighting, it's more of a party compound than a cart. Serving up unusual variations on the classic grilled-cheese sandwich, this is party central on weekends.

This is also home of the Cheesus Burger: a fully loaded hamburger that uses grilled-cheese sandwiches as the buns (so named when one of his friends, served the burger for the first time, exclaimed, "Cheesus!"). Grilled Cheese Grill is opening up a new location at SE 28th and Ankeny, featuring a restored double-decker bus as seating and another Airstream for the kitchen. Willamette Week's Best of Portland 2010 listed the Grilled Cheese Grill as a runner-up for Best Place to Pick Up a Date.

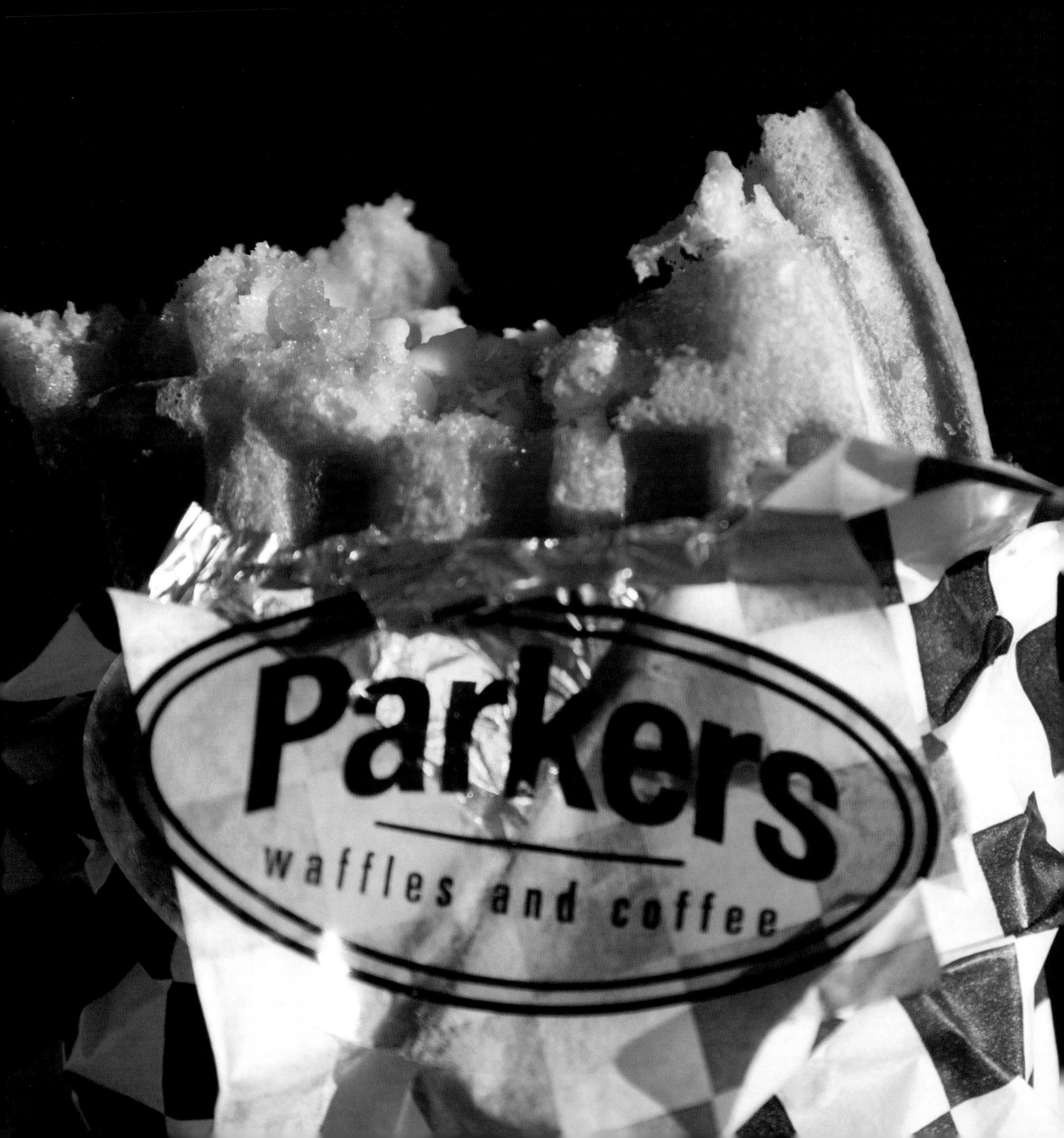
ParKers
waffles and coffee

ABBIE & SCOTT TRIMBLE
Parkers Waffles

Abbie and Scott are a hungry couple. Shortly after moving to Portland in 2000, Abbie dreamed of starting her own cart. She loved food and thought she could make a living from her passion, but Scott said it would never work. When she started talking about waffles, and the prospect of transforming waffles into a food that would be suitable for any meal of the day, Scott reconsidered, and they got to work. Abbie and Scott decided to base their entire food cart concept around the waffle, believing it to be a creation of the gods. "It's a blank canvas!" Abbie exclaims enthusiastically. Scott admits that he didn't know Abbie was a waffle genius when they first hooked up. "I thought she was cool, but I had no idea this monster was lurking just beneath the surface."

How has marriage, two kids, and working side by side in a food cart affected their relationship? "It's literally the best thing we could have done together," Scott says. "We haven't had sex in six months, but I'm happier. I think I am. Right, baby?"

"We chose our first location at Portland State University because we liked the energy of the students. Besides, we thought the grid would subconsciously be attractive to the engineering students across the street," they explain. " Our second location on Alberta Street was chosen for much the same reason. It's an incredibly vibrant area, popular for its art scene, great for nightlife, and a very family-friendly neighborhood."

What Abbie and Scott love about owning a food cart are their customers. "I don't know what it is about the waffle, but it really brings out the best in people," says Abbie.

DISTRICT: NORTH PORTLAND

MISSISSIPPI MARKETPLACE

Location:
N. Mississippi and Skidmore, adjacent to Prost

Description:
The first purpose-built food cart development, created by Roger Goldingay, the Mississippi Marketplace is clustered around a German-style pub called Prost and is home to about ten food carts.

Best Time of Day:
Daily brunch and lunch

Types of Food:
Vegan and vegetarian fare, Italian street food, breakfast sandwiches, sushi, dessert/gorgeous baked goods, coffee, Mediterranean, New Mexican/Southwestern, roasted nuts, pizza, Thai, rice bowls, falafel

FOOD PROFILE / DISTRICT: NORTH

The Big Egg

MISSISSIPPI MARKETPLACE: N. Mississippi & Skidmore

On the one hand, a breakfast sandwich isn't really that big of a deal. Eggs, bread, meat, cheese… and voilà. But in the hands of the folks at the Big Egg, it is a truly sublime creation. Take The Portlander, with hardwood-smoked bacon or Black Forest ham, Tillamook white cheddar, fontina, or gorgonzola, and fresh chive and country Dijon mustard on a grilled Grand Central Bakery brioche. They make everything fresh to order, so your best bet is to sit back with a nice hot cup of joe from the cart next door, Dogfeathers, and wake up a bit before you tuck into your sandwich. We don't know of a much better way to start the day in Portland.

NORTH PORTLAND

N. VANCOUVER AVENUE AND FREMONT STREET

Location:
N. Vancouver Avenue and Fremont Street

Description:
This abandoned gas-station site began as a food cart pod with a coffee drive-through/bike-through. This first coffee cart was replaced by Hava Java, and then joined by Mum's and Quesabrosa. The two wings of the former gas station provide shelter for diners eating at picnic benches. Inside the structure is a dry-cleaning operation and a shoe-repair shop, making this pod one of the first mixed-use pod developments.

Best Time of Day:
Daily breakfast through early dinner

Types of Food:
South African/Indian, Mexican, coffee

REFUEL STATION NORTH

Location:
N. Greeley Avenue and Killingsworth Street

Description:
This is the second purpose-built food cart pod in Portland (after Mississippi Marketplace). Located on a busy main street that cuts through the Overlook neighborhood, this pod is family oriented and packed with delicious fare. The pod shares a parking lot and indoor and outdoor seating with Pizza Depokos. This is one of the few pods where you can have a beer with your food—as long as you stay within the designated areas.

Best Time of Day:
Most days and evenings, gets hopping Thursday and Friday at dinner and all day Saturday and Sunday

Types of Food:
Lots of gluten-free, vegetarian, and vegan options, Korean street food, BBQ, steamed burgers, salads, waffles, Guamanian, Venezuelan, mac and cheese, Thai, organic ice cream, soup, baked goods

TIMBER ADAMSON & ALI CLARYS

Yogio

Chef Timber began her restaurant career at the age of fifteen. For years, she worked in restaurants and cooked for her friends on the side while she pursued her main career goals in graphic design and photography. Struggling to find work in that field, she began researching culinary schools, and ended up at Portland's Western Culinary Institute. She went on to further refine her cooking skills at world-class haute-cuisine restaurant Alinea in Chicago before returning to the Portland area. On a hiatus from cooking, she traveled extensively in Southeast Asia and delved into traditional Korean cooking. And it's lucky for Portland that she did. After her return she and Yogio business partner Ali Clarys were laid off from other jobs and decided the time was right to launch their gourmet Korean food cart. Their goal is to bring to Portland old Korean dishes that have never been seen or experienced by most of America, and to show Portland that there is so much more to Korea than just barbecue.

CRYSTAL FOOD GARDEN

Location:
N. Richmond Avenue at Lombard Street

Description:
At the gateway of the St. John's neighborhood, in a freshly paved parking lot next to the Crystal Temple, is one of Portland's newer pods. At press time, there were only three carts, but there are a dozen slots and several are scheduled to open soon.

Best Time of Day:
A little early to tell, but appears to be daily lunchtime and early dinner

Types of Food:
Korean fusion, southern, pizza, Coney Island dogs, Vietnamese pho, tamales

NORTH PORTLAND:
NOTABLE LONER CARTS

FLAVOUR SPOT

Locations:
1. N. Lombard between Denver and Greeley,
2. N. Mississippi and Fremont Street,
3. pod location at SW Third and Washington

Best time of day:
Weekend breakfast through late afternoon

Flavour Spot claims to serve the "Original Portland Dutch Taco," that is, waffle-wraps with fillings that range from Nutella and bananas to cream cheese and berries. Decadent and delicious.

NOTABLE LONER CARTS:
NORTH PORTLAND

CHE CAFÉ

Location:
N. Williams and Shaver Street

Best time of day:
Daily lunch

Che Café is a shiny red cart with outdoor seating in the neighboring courtyard, where you can feast under the shade of an old willow tree. The menu includes soup, mac and cheese, tofu fries, pulled-pork sandwiches, meatloaf, burgers, homemade ketchup, and more.

KING BURRITO

Location:
N. Mississippi Avenue at Failing Street

Best Time of Day:
Daily lunch and early dinner

A food cart veteran of over fourteen years, King Burrito owner Jose Alvarez decided to leave one of the oldest pods in town at SW Fifth and Oak to move up north to Mississippi Avenue. He has expanded his menu and now features ice cream and handcrafted drinks along with his signature burritos. Why did he move? He claims, "There are too many Mexican carts down there now."

CONTRIBUTORS

ANDREW BURDICK specializes in long-term photojournalistic storytelling and creative writing. His work focuses on the ever-evolving relationship between people, the world in which we live, and the natural systems we depend on for survival, security, and happiness. Using images as an educational and storytelling tool, he aims to help reconnect people with our environments in order to promote a necessary culture of stewardship for people, life, and the planet. More of his work can be found at: andrewburdickphotography.com.

BRETT BURMEISTER, a lifelong Portlander, ate at his first food cart back in 1991 during a college trip into the city. That first Honkin' Huge burrito from Shelly's Garden in Pioneer Courthouse Square made Brett a believer. He has been evangelizing the glories of Portland's street food ever since. Over those nineteen years, Brett has introduced skeptical coworkers, visiting guests, and even close family to the downtown carts. Whether it be Hawaiian bento or Thai noodles or the famous Schnitzelwic from Tábor, Brett has eaten there. Brett began writing about the city on several blogs, including Portland Metblogs and OurPDX. He combined his love of writing with his passion for food carts when he joined Lizzy Caston at Food Carts Portland in 2008. Since then, Brett has taken over the daily management of the website and become the unofficial ambassador of Portland's food carts. FoodCartsPortland.com has been featured on CNN, and in the *New York Times*, the *Los Angeles Times* and *Gourmet* magazine as the source for all matters related to Portland's food carts. Brett is what the cart owners refer to as a Cartivore and he wears that title proudly. Most days, you can find Brett wandering through the city visiting the different pods and sampling the tasty items on offer.

HANNAH CARLEN is a music publicist and occasional freelance writer living in Portland, OR. Her primary professional focus is publicity geared toward college and public radio programming. A native New Yorker, Hannah became a food enthusiast in college, and expanded her palette through travel and waitressing. Her favorite foods are those that bring a little rusticity to complex, elevated flavors, so her love of Portland food and food carts comes as no surprise. Hannah hopes to launch a supermarket blog in 2011.

PAUL GERALD's writing career began at the sports desks of various daily newspapers in the South, where he grew up. Since then, he's been a freelance travel, outdoors, and sports writer, and his articles have appeared in the *Memphis Flyer*, *Northwest Airlines' WorldTraveler*, *Willamette Week* and *The Oregonian*. He's also worked in landscaping, restaurants, public relations, social work, an amusement park, Alaskan fishing boats, the YMCA, corporate marketing, and as a package handler for FedEx. Such is the life of a writer who really, really wants to avoid having a regular job. He wrote *60 Hikes Within 60 Miles of Portland* (the fourth edition came out in 2010) and *Day and Overnight Hikes: Oregon's Pacific Crest Trail*, and he revised *Best Tent Camping: Oregon for its 2009* second edition. He's even become his own publisher, putting out *Breakfast in Bridgetown: The Definitive Guide to Portland's Favorite Meal* in 2008, under the name Bacon and Eggs Press. And he now hosts a weekly internet radio show of the same title for PDX.FM. Basically, he likes to go to interesting places, do fun stuff, eat, and write about it. Getting paid for such things seems like quite the benefit.

CAROL MAYER-REED, FASLA, is a partner with Portland-based design firm Mayer/Reed. As a landscape architect and urban designer, she designs parks, waterfronts, streetscapes, college campuses, and public open spaces in the Pacific Northwest. Carol is intrigued by the evolution of street vendors in Portland. She is particularly interested in studying how the food cart phenomenon has activated the public realm, how it has created vitality out of vacant and underutilized space, and its positive social effects on the street life of Portland's downtown and its neighborhoods.

MICHAEL REED is a partner with Portland-based design firm Mayer/Reed. As a product and graphic designer, he designs wayfinding and signage programs for public spaces associated with streetscapes, public transit, cultural facilities, university and corporate campuses in the United States. Michael is engaged with how visual communication informs users and defines place in the built environment. He is interested in how clusters of food carts located in vacant lots and parking lots contribute to the character of neighborhoods through the materials, site amenities, and iconographic elements they employ.

REFERENCES

Abbott, Carl. *Greater Portland: Urban life and landscape in the Pacific Northwest*. Philadelphia: University of Pennsylvania Press, 2001.

Burningham, Lucy. "Portland Food Carts Push Through Recession." *Oregon Business*, January 2010. http://www.oregonbusiness.com/articles/78-january-2010/2775-cash-and-carry.

Chastain, April. "Food Carts as Retail Real Estate." *PSU Center for Real Estate, Quarterly & Urban Development Journal*, 2nd quarter 2010.

Givot, Scott. Personal communication, May 20, 2010.

Gross, Matt. "Frugal Portland." *New York Times*, May 10, 2009. http://travel.nytimes.com/2009/05/10/travel/10portland.html.

Jacobs, Jane. *The Death and Life of Great American Cities*. New York: Random House, 1961.

LaFarge, Albert, ed. *The Essential William H. Whyte*. New York: Fordham University Press, 2000.

Langdon, Philip. "Food carts take the curse off Portland's parking lots." *New Urban News*, January/February 2010.

Merrill, Jessica. "In Oregon, It´s a Brew Pub World." *New York Times*, January 13, 2006. http://travel.nytimes.com/2006/01/13/travel/escapes/13beer.html.

Peat, Don. "Food Carts Can Be Good Business." *Toronto Sun*, August 31, 2009. http://www.torontosun.com/news/torontoandgta/2009/08/31/10683596-sun.html

Putnam, Robert D. and Lewis M. Feldstein with Don Cohen. *Better Together: Restoring the American Community*. New York: Simon and Schuster, 2003.

Robertson-Textor, Marisa. "The Gourmet Q+A: Sean Basinski." *Gourmet*, September 25, 2009, http://www.gourmet.com/food/2009/09/sean-basinkski-vendy-awards.

Tinker, Irene. *Street Foods: Urban food and employment in developing countries*. New York: Oxford University Press, 1997

Urban Vitality Group. *Food Cartology: Rethinking Urban Spaces as People Spaces*. No date. www.portlandonline.com/shared/cfm/image.cfm?id+200738